Joseph Mitchell

MY EARS ARE BENT

Joseph Mitchell came to New York City in 1929 from a small farming town called Fairmont, in the swamp country of southeastern North Carolina. He was twenty-one years old. He worked as a reporter and feature writer—for *The World*, *The New York Herald Tribune*, and *The New York World-Telegram*—for eight years, and then went to *The New Yorker*, where he worked off and on until his death in 1996.

Books by Joseph Mitchell

My Ears Are Bent

McSorley's Wonderful Saloon

Old Mr. Flood

The Bottom of the Harbor

Joe Gould's Secret

Up in the Old Hotel

MY EARS
ARE BENT

Joseph Mitchell

VINTAGE BOOKS

A Division of Random House, Inc.

New York

FIRST VINTAGE BOOKS EDITION, JULY 2008

The photographs appearing on pages xv and 301 are by Therese
Mitchell. Copyright © The Estate of Joseph Mitchell.

The pieces in this collection were originally published, sometimes
in somewhat different form, in the *New York World-Telegram*,
the *New York Herald Tribune*, and *The New Yorker*.

The Library of Congress has cataloged the Pantheon edition as follows:
Mitchell, Joseph, 1908–1996.
My ears are bent / Joseph Mitchell.
p. cm.
1. New York (N.Y.)—Social life and customs—20th century.
2. New York (N.Y.)—Biography. 3. Interviews—
New York (State)—New York. I. Title.
F128.5 .M718 2001   974.7'1091—dc21   00-053742
ISBN: 978-0-375-72630-9

Book design by Fearn Cutler de Vicq

www.vintagebooks.com

FOR
WILLIAM HARRY MITCHELL
AND FLORENCE MITCHELL

Contents

CONTENTS

Foreword

Joseph Mitchell worked as a reporter and feature writer for *The World, The Herald Tribune,* and *The World-Telegram* from 1929, when he arrived in New York, until 1938, when he joined *The New Yorker.* Mitchell's apprenticeship as a writer began on newspapers, and those early years as a newspaperman defined him for the rest of his life. He always referred to himself as "a reporter" and called *The New Yorker* "the paper."

My Ears Are Bent, a selection of Mitchell's feature stories and articles from *The Herald Tribune* and *The World-Telegram,* first appeared in 1938. In 1992, when Mitchell collected much of his published work in *Up in the Old Hotel,* he chose not to include *My Ears Are Bent,* despite the fact that it had been out of print for over half a century. He explained his decision in one simple sentence: "It was a different kind of writing."

This new edition of *My Ears Are Bent* contains most

of Mitchell's original stories from the first edition, but more important is the inclusion here of a number of stories from the same period that have not been available since he first wrote them. Working as a "district man" at *The Herald Tribune,* Mitchell covered Brooklyn, the West Side of Manhattan, and Harlem. On the advice of one of his early editors, he lived in rooming houses all over the city, getting to know each neighborhood a few weeks at a time. As a feature writer for *The World-Telegram,* he went farther afield, roaming through Staten Island, the Bronx, and Queens, especially the waterfronts and riversides.

We can see in these pieces the genesis of many of Mitchell's later stories. Here we catch our first glimpse of Mazie, the philanthropic ticket-taker at the Venice Theatre. Here too, we read of his initial encounters with Father Divine, which led to his fascination with street preachers and urban evangelists. "Saltwater Farmers" presages "Dragger Captain" and "The Rivermen" in *The Bottom of the Harbor.*

At *The World-Telegram* Mitchell, like all feature writers, interviewed many a celebrity. He wrote a series on Eleanor Roosevelt, and one on the anthropologist Franz Boas, whom he greatly admired. He interviewed Albert Einstein and Emma Goldman. He filed a series of stories on the trial of Bruno Hauptmann, the notorious kidnapper of the Lindbergh baby.

And he also interviewed many people connected with the theater and the other performing arts—Bing Crosby, Rudy Vallee, Helen Morgan, Tallulah Bankhead, Noël Coward, Fats Waller, Clara Bow.

We have added a final section, entitled "Showmanship," because it embodies the kinds of stories Mitchell never wrote again: a piece on the young Gene Krupa, an interview with an aging George M. Cohan, and Mitchell's hilarious and iconoclastic takes on the great playwright George Bernard Shaw.

This edition of *My Ears Are Bent,* we hope, makes clear that Mitchell's later work at *The New Yorker* was the direct result of the early years he spent learning his craft, educating himself as a writer and studying every aspect of what came to be his obsession—the waterways and byways, the hidden crevices and corners, the majestic anomalies of New York City and the people in it.

Sheila McGrath
Dan Frank
January 2001

Portrait of the author

MY EARS ARE BENT

CHAPTER I

My Ears Are Bent

Except for a period in 1931 when I got sick of the whole business and went to sea, working on a freighter which carried heavy machinery to Leningrad and brought Soviet pulp logs back, I have been for the last eight years a reporter on newspapers in New York City. In the summer after I left the University of North Carolina in 1929 I had an appendix operation and while getting over it I read James Bryce's "American Commonwealth," a book which made me want to become a political reporter. I came to New York City with that idea in mind. The first story I remember covering was a Jack the Ripper murder in a Brooklyn apartment house; an old woman had been strangled with a silk stocking and cut to death in her bedroom, the walls of which were virtually covered with large, lascivious photographs.

I was a "district man" at night for The Herald

Tribune. I sat in an easy chair which had fleas in it in an old tenement across the street from Police Headquarters in Brooklyn hour after hour, waiting for something violent to happen. All the newspapers had offices in the tenement. When something happened the man on the desk at Headquarters would let us know and we would leave our tenement offices and hurry to the scene of the murder, or stick-up, or wreck, or brawl, or fire, or whatever. Then we would telephone the news in to a rewrite man. I covered districts for about four months. I covered Brooklyn, the West Side of Manhattan, and Harlem. I liked Harlem best.

In Harlem the reporters had a shack—the district man calls his office "the shack"—on the ground floor of the Hotel Theresa, the biggest hotel in Harlem, and we used to sit in the doorway in swivel chairs and look out at the people passing to and fro on Seventh Avenue, Harlem's main street. There were four reporters in Harlem at night, three from the morning papers and one from the City News Association. My colleagues were veterans. The thing they disliked most in a reporter was enthusiasm, and I was always excited. When I got on the telephone to give my office a story—in the booth I used to try to balance the telephone receiver on my left shoulder the way they did, but I never succeeded—they would stand outside and point at their foreheads and make circles in the air, indicating that I did not have any sense. We would take turns making the rounds of the police stations. On the rounds we would sometimes drop into a speakeasy or a night club or a gambling flat and try to pull a story out of it. I got to know a few underworld figures and I used to like to listen to them talk.

One was Gilligan Holton, a Negro who ran a honky-tonk of the "intimate" type—it was in a basement—which he called the Broken Leg and Busted, a saloon name surpassed only by the Heat Wave Bar & Grill, a more recent establishment. When I worked in Harlem many wealthy men and women from downtown got drunk up there every night and Holton had a quantity of information about them, some of which would gag a goat. I remember one well-heeled woman who used to come to his basement place; she was in the habit of having Negro men, mostly tap-dancers, examined by a doctor before she had affairs with them. She had a grown daughter. I used to see this old sister and her grown daughter slobbering around the Harlem bars every night. Until I came to New York City I had never lived in a town with a population of more than 2,699, and I was alternately delighted and frightened out of my wits by what I saw at night in Harlem. I would go off duty at 3 A.M., and then I would walk around the streets and look, discovering what the depression and the prurience of white men were doing to a people who are "last to be hired; first to be fired." When I got tired of looking, usually around daybreak, I would get on the subway and go to my $9 a week furnished room in Greenwich Village. When I got out of the subway at Sheridan Square I would get a Herald Tribune to see what the rewrite man had done with the stories I had telephoned in hours earlier. I had a police card in my pocket and I was twenty-one years old and everything was new to me. By the time the Harlem trick was over I was so fascinated by the melodrama of the metropolis at night that I forgot my ambition to become a political reporter.

Harlem was the last district I covered. After that I was brought into the city room and allowed to write my own stories. I worked under Stanley Walker, a slight, calm but unpredictable Texan, who was the most celebrated city editor of the period. I did general assignments, mostly crime. The only kind of crime I liked was gangster funerals and they threw a lot of big ones that year. Crime, especially murder, was difficult to cover on The Herald Tribune because we were under orders to avoid the use of the word "blood" in a story. One of the owners did not like that word. On some stories it was impossible to be sufficiently exquisite. For example, I remember going down to a speakeasy on Elizabeth Street to cover the throat-slitting of a petty gangster. It was one of those speakeasies with artificial grapevines wired to the booths. After his throat had been cut this gangster had crawled out of his booth and stumbled all over the place, losing blood with each stumble. The little establishment looked as if blood had been shot in through a hose. . . .

I got tired of hoofing after dime-a-dozen murders—that year it seemed that all the people in the metropolitan area were trying to murder each other—and one morning I went downtown and got a job as a deck boy on a worn-out Hog Island freighter, the City of Fairbury. We tied up in Leningrad for fourteen days. Two of us met some freckled, brown-eyed girls who worked on the docks—even the winch-drivers were girls—and took them to a Charlie Chaplin movie in a theater on the Prospekt of the Twenty-fifth of October. The girl I was with would give me a nudge in the guts with her elbow and bellow with laughter every time Chaplin fell on his face, and it was one of his roller-skating films. Next day the two girls got us all tickets on the railroad to Detskoie Selo, which used to be the summer residence of the Czar's family but now is a rest home for workers and their children. It is south of Leningrad and the flat, swampy country reminded me of eastern North Carolina. Somewhere on the tremendous estate the two girls picked some wild strawberries, and that night they made some cakes, a wild Russian strawberry on the top of each cake. We ate them and got sick.

I remember how proud they were when they put the cakes on the table, smiling at us, and how ashamed we were, an hour or so later, when we got sick. We figured out it was the change in the water, but we couldn't explain that to them because we knew no Russian. In Leningrad we swam naked each day in the Neva, under the gentle Russian sun. One afternoon we got together, the seamen from all the American ships in the harbor, and marched with the Russians in a demonstration against imperialist war, an annual event. One night a girl invited me to her house and I had dinner with her family, thick cabbage soup and black bread which smelled of wet grain. After dinner the family sang. The girl knew some English and she asked me to sing an American song. I favored them with the only one I could think of, "Body and Soul," which was popular in New York City when I left. It seemed to puzzle them.

I left the freighter when it docked in the Port of Albany, New York, to unload its cargo of pulp logs. I took a bus to New York City, and a few weeks later I got a job on The World-Telegram, an afternoon newspaper, where I still work. Most of the time I have been assigned to write feature stories and interviews and in the course of this assignment I have been tortured by some of the fanciest ear-benders in the world, including George Bernard Shaw and the noted ever-voluble educator Nicholas Murray Butler, and I have long since lost the ability to detect insanity. Sometimes it is necessary for me to go into a psychopathic ward on a story and I never notice the difference. In a newspaper office no day is typical, but I will describe one day no more incoherent than a hundred others. When I came in one morning at 9 I was assigned to find and interview an Italian bricklayer who resembled the Prince of Wales; someone telephoned that he had been offered a job in Hollywood. I tracked him to the cellar of a matzoth bakery on the East Side, where he was repairing an oven. I got into a fight with the man who ran the bakery; he thought I was an inspector from the Health Department. I finally got to the bricklayer and he would not talk much about himself but kept saying, "I'm afraid I get sued." I went back to my office and wrote that story and then I was assigned to get an interview with a lady boxer who was living at the St. Moritz Hotel. She had all her boxing equipment in her room. The room smelled of sweat and wet leather, reminding me of the locker-room of Philadelphia Jack O'Brien's gym on a rainy day. She told me she was not only a lady boxer but a Countess as well. Then she put on gloves to show me how she fought and if I had not crawled under the bed she would have knocked my head off. "I'm a ball of fire," she yelled. I went back to the office and wrote that story and then I was assigned to interview Samuel J. Burger, who had telephoned my office that he was selling racing cock-roaches to society people at seventy-five cents a pair. Mr. Burger is the theatrical agent who booked such attractions as the late John Dillinger's father, a suc-cession of naked dancers, and Mrs. Jack (Legs) Dia-mond. He once tried to book the entire Hauptmann jury. I found him in a delicatessen on Broadway where he was buying combination ham and cheese sand-wiches for a couple of strip-tease women. He pulled out a check made out to him and proved that he had sold and delivered a consignment of cockroaches to a society matron who planned to enliven a party with them, the cute thing. Mr. Burger said he had estab-lished a service called Ballyhoo Associates through which he rented animals to people. "I rent a lot of monkeys," he told me. "People get lonesome and telephone me to send them a monkey to keep them company. After all, a monkey is a mammal, just like us." I wrote that story and then I went home. An-other day another dollar.

Do not get the idea, however, that I am outraged by ear-benders. The only people I do not care to listen to are society women, industrial leaders, dis-tinguished authors, ministers, explorers, moving pic-ture actors (except W. C. Fields and Stepin Fetchit), and any actress under the age of thirty-five. I believe the most interesting human beings, so far as talk is concerned, are anthropologists, farmers, prostitutes, psychiatrists, and an occasional bartender. The best talk is artless, the talk of people trying to reassure or comfort themselves, women in the sun, grouped around baby carriages, talking about their weeks in the hospital or the way meat has gone up, or men in saloons, talking to combat the loneliness everyone feels. The talk when you interview someone for a newspaper is usually premeditated and usually artificial.

Now and then, however, someone says something so unexpected it is magnificent. Once I was working on a series of stories about voodoo and black magic in New York City. With an assistant district attorney, I had a long talk with a Negro streetwalker. From the vague story she told the Vice Squad detective who put her in the pokey the D.A. suspected that she had been used as an altar in a black mass. She wasn't much help because she saw nothing particularly unusual in her experience. Finally, exasperated, the D.A. asked her why she became a prostitute in the first place, and she said, "I just wanted to be accommodating."

You seldom know what you are going to ask about when you are sent to interview someone. The desk says, "Go interview this dope," and you locate the person and start talking. It has to be done in a hurry and there are few people who can just open their mouths and say something worth printing in a newspaper. Usually the best way to start an interview with a well-known person is to recall the worst thing you ever heard about him and ask if it is true. You have to make a person angry but not too angry. I remember the icy glint that came into the eyes of Aimee Semple McPherson when I asked her if it was true that she ordained her husband, David L. Hutton, a stout torch singer, so he could get passes on the railroad. That is not always the best way. Whenever I have to interview Mrs. Ella A. Boole, the world president of the W.C.T.U., I give her to understand that I am a far greater enemy of rum than she is.

Some people—Gertrude Stein, Emma Goldman, Gilda Gray, Eleanor Holm and Peter J. McGuinness, Sheriff of Brooklyn, are an assortment—can unload enough quotes for a story at any hour of the day or night. (Gilda Gray, the Polish shimmy-shaker, is nice. Once I went up to see her about a rumored engagement to some scion or other. She sensed there was no particular story in that and told me instead about a visit she made to the convent in Milwaukee in which she was educated. She had lunch with the nuns and before they sat down to eat she gave them a few movements of the black bottom, a dance from the twenties. "I gave the sisters a few tosses just for old time's sake," said Miss Gray. "They sure did enjoy it.") Two classes of humans whose quotes are always amusing are frustrated, spiteful old actresses on the down grade and people with phobias, especially people who predict the end of the world. (There used to be a disappointed man named Robert Reidt out on Long Island who was always going up on a hilltop near East Patchogue with his family to await destruction. Predicting the end of the world was an obsession with him. One dull day I called him up to ask if he had any advance information on the crack of doom and the telephone operator said, "Mr. Reidt's telephone has been disconnected.") A woman whose conversation was always unpremeditated was the late Mary Louise Cecilia (Texas) Guinan. Once I went with her to Flushing where she and her "Gang of Twenty Beautiful Guinan Girls" were filling a vaudeville engagement. We rode out in her bullet-proof limousine, an automobile previously owned by Larry Fay, the cutthroat. Someone was planning to produce a play based on the life of Aimee Semple McPherson and Miss Guinan had been asked to play the lead. I remarked that Mrs. McPherson certainly would sue the producer. "That," said Miss Guinan, "is no skin off my ass."

I am pleased when an interview starts off like that. I admire the imagery in vulgar conversation. I wish newspapers had courage enough to print conversation just as it issues forth, relevant obscenity and all. Some of Mayor La Guardia's most apt epigrams, for example, cannot be printed in any New York newspaper. If a reporter tries to get anything unusually hearty in a story some copyreader or other will trim it out. There are scores of admirable copyreaders on New York newspapers, but most of them seem to be too bored to give much of a damn about anything. They don't have to be censored; they willingly censor themselves. They appear to prefer the nasty genteelism to the exact word; they will cut the word "belly" out of your copy and write in the nauseating word "tummy." I have seen a pimp referred to as "a representative of the vice ring." On the newspaper for which I work the reporters write "raped" and it always comes out "criminally attacked." Also, copyreaders appear to like tinsel words, words such as "petite." Day after day in one newspaper I have seen Lottie Coll referred to as "the petite gun-girl," and Lottie is as big as Jack Dempsey and twice as tough. A good copyreader would rip a word like "petite" off a sheet of copy just on general principles. Once I covered a political rally at which a tipsy statesman cursed his opponent for fifteen violent minutes. His profanity was so vigorous I expected it to leave cavities in his teeth. I used some of his milder remarks in my story, but the copyreader cut it out and wrote in, "Commissioner Etcetera declared that his opponent was not aware of the issues." There is no fury which can equal the black fury which bubbles up in a reporter when he sees his name signed to a story which has been castrated by a copyreader or one of the officials on the city desk.

The least interesting people to interview for an afternoon newspaper are the ones who probably should be the most interesting, industrial leaders, automobile manufacturers, Wall Street financiers, oil and steel czars, people like that. They either chew your ears off with nonsense about how they are self-made ("When I landed in this country all I had was seventeen cents and a poppyseed roll and now I am chairman of the board") or they sit around and look gloomy. After painfully interviewing one of those gentlemen you go down in the elevator and walk into the street and see the pretty girls, the pretty working girls, with their jolly breasts bouncing about under their dresses and you are relieved; you feel as if you had escaped from a tomb in which the worms were just beginning their work; you feel that it would be better to cheat, lie, steal, stick up drugstores or stretch out dead drunk in the gutter than to end up like one of those industrial leaders with a face that looks like a bowl of cold oatmeal. Next down the list are society women. I rank them with the jimson-weed and the vermiform appendix; I cannot see any reason for their existence. Also, they have bad manners. In the line of duty I have had dealings with scores of drunken dowagers and gawky, concupiscent debutantes and it is my belief that the society women of the United States have the worst manners of any women in the world; coffeepot waitresses are gracious in comparison.

Politicians, as a rule, make work easy for the reporter. Some of them are so entertaining you can write about them under water. (Herbert Hoover is not in this class. He is the gloomy kind. I have interviewed him twice and both times his face kept reminding me of the face of a fat baby troubled by gas pains.) It is perhaps an ugly commentary on the American press, but the function of the interviewer on most newspapers is to entertain, not to shed light. For his purposes, men like Huey Long and Hyman Schorenstein, a Brooklyn district leader who is reputed to be unable to read or write, are made to order. An interviewer soon begins to judge public figures on the basis of their entertainment value, overlooking their true importance. It is not easy to get an interview with Professor Franz Boas, the greatest anthropologist in the world, across a city desk, but a mild interview with Oom the Omnipotent will hit the bottom of page one under a two-column head. Also, the American press will string along with the fatuous, attacking only the weak and the eccentric. Even the semicolons are pompous on Nicholas Murray Butler's mimeographed statements, but the papers nail them to the front page practically every Monday morning in the year. If Nicholas Murray Butler and Peter J. McGuinness made the same identical statement the papers would treat Mr. Butler with a gigantic amount of respect but Pete would be treated as a yap who should keep his mouth shut. It is safe to write accurately only about the nuts and the bums. When a public figure does something ridiculous reporters may then write about him accurately. J. P. Morgan was always treated with elaborate respect until he played rock-a-bye-baby with a lady midget; then the newspapers were not afraid of him any more.

Huey Long, as I say, was made to order. Any barely literate reporter could write an epic about him. The last time I saw him he was sitting up in bed in the Waldorf-Astoria with a hangover. He had on a pair of baby-blue pajamas and he was yawning and scratching his toes. There were three reporters in the room asking him questions. To every question he would say, "It's a lie," and laugh throatily. Then he sat on the edge of the bed, groaning, and told a long incoherent story about a relative of his who kept a saloon. The politician most lavish with incoherent quotes, however, was former Mayor John P. O'Brien of New York City. It was worth money to hear him orate. Once I heard him speak to a gathering of women and he said, "During the week I have momentous matters to attend to. I meet great people and I must go here and there to make up the addenda that goes with being Mayor of the city. Therefore when I come here to this great forum and see before me flowers and buds, ladies, girls and widows, emotion is just running riot with me." Another time he got to his feet and said, "Mr. President, and may I say, brothers? When I get in a room with chairs I get the fraternal spirit." Once he addressed the Ohio Society and he read a poem, sighed and said, "I yearn now and then for the dear old river or for some Bohemia where you can get away from the stress of it all." I have seen a puzzled audience staring at him, wondering what he was getting at. One night I listened to him tell about the time he almost slid off the tailboard of a furniture van and I was so fascinated by the words tumbling out of his mouth that I forgot to take notes. After his speech I went up to a stenographer he had brought there himself and got him to read me off a hunk of the oration. We printed the story next day and two of his campaign managers came around and said I made the whole thing up and threatened to sue for $150,000.

No reporter can work on interviews constantly without becoming a little batty; sooner or later he will begin hearing the birdies sing. When it gets through with more important matters I think that rotation of jobs should be one of the points taken up by the American Newspaper Guild, the union of newspapermen, of which I am a member and in whose program I believe. When a city editor catches you looking cross-eyed at your notes and wishing black plagues on the head of the inarticulate lulu you have just interviewed he is sometimes nice enough to put you on the street for a while, or on rewrite, or maybe a big story breaks and saves your sanity. Just when you are about to collapse with one of the occupational diseases of the reporter—indigestion, alcoholism, cynicism and Nicholas Murray Butler are a few of them—a big story, a blood-hunt that takes you out of the office, usually breaks.

I was once saved by the Hauptmann trial. In rapid succession I had interviewed a crooner making a come-back, an injured trapeze performer, the proprietor of a lonely hearts bureau, a student of earthquakes, a woman undertaker, a man who manufactures the fans used by fan dancers, a champion blood donor and Samuel Goldwyn, and had begun to whimper when I got near a typewriter. Then I was sent to Flemington, New Jersey, to write courtroom features during Hauptmann's trial. The trial was a nightmare to most of the reporters who covered it and before it was over I had begun to talk in the unknown tongue, but at first it was soothing not to have to ask questions but to sit still and listen to those asked by the Attorney General of the State of New Jersey.

Compared with most newspaper work a trial is easy to cover—that is, a murder trial; a thing like the Bank of United States trial is another matter. A financial trial is slow torture. At a murder trial you simply sit still and write down what happens. After a reporter has covered features for a while there is nothing like a fast murder trial to get the lead out of his pants. It discourages him from trying to make literature out of every little two-by-four news story; a newspaper can have no bigger nuisance than a reporter who is always trying to write literature.

My office had at least ten reporters in Flemington through all the addled weeks of the Hauptmann trial—compared with our competitors we were understaffed—and we covered it better than any other afternoon newspaper. We were able to do so because each night when court adjourned we left the fevered atmosphere of Flemington, where reporters were as enforcedly gregarious as fishing-worms in a can, and did not return until court opened next morning.

Throughout the trial we lived in Stockton, New Jersey, ten miles or so from Flemington, in a small hotel, the Stockton, which was established in 1832 and which is celebrated for its hearty American grub, things like breasts of chicken with thick slices of red, sugar-cured ham. We took over the establishment and installed a night wire downstairs. The hotel is operated by five brothers and their mother, the

Colligans. One of the brothers has a daughter who once won a prize in the Irish Sweepstakes. The hotel is a block from the Delaware River, and the Delaware toting ice is one of the most stirring spectacles I have seen. It makes you feel religious, or patriotic, or something. We used to go down there at night and watch slabs of ice as big as box-cars piling up against the bridge pillars; late at night we could stand on the porch of the hotel and hear the crunch of the ice in the river. There is a canal on each bank of the Delaware and they froze solid and we used to go down with two little sleds owned by the hotel and take belly-whoppers on the ice. Next morning we would eat great stacks of pancakes and Philadelphia scrapple and rashers of Mrs. Colligan's red ham. I enjoyed the sledding in Stockton; it was the last exercise I had until the following winter, when I got in an airplane wreck near Cleveland after flying over the flooded Ohio River valley.

The hotel kept its groceries out back in a cave torn out of the side of a hill. In the cave was a big barrel containing 180 red-legged terrapin which William Colligan, the eldest brother, had snatched out of a mountain stream in Sussex County. We had terrapin stew every night for a week, a stew made with sherry. After that we just played with the terrapin; someone would bring an armful of the terrapin into the bar every night. We had a lot of visitors in

Stockton. Each weekend our wives came out. One stormy night Thomas Benton, the painter, came out. He had been sent to make sketches at the trial by my newspaper. When he saw our oak fire he pulled off his shoes and sat down in front of it and talked until midnight about the beauty of the United States.

After dinner each night we had to leave the crowd in the bar—there were two bars in the hotel; one for the local farmers, one for the guests of the hotel— and go upstairs and write our "overnights," stories written to run only until the trial got under way next day. That is, they would run in the Home and Twelve O'Clock editions and be thrown out of the Night. Everybody used one room, a big room with a fire-place in it, and by 10 P.M. the room would be full of cursing reporters whacking out nonsense on por-table typewriters. Wesley Price, who acted as a sort of walking city editor during the trial, would go from typewriter to typewriter, snatching out takes of copy. He would look at the stuff, groan, and send it down, sheet by sheet, to the sleepy telegraph operator he had stationed in the hotel office. Girls from Trenton and Philadelphia used to come to Stockton at night and they would stand in the door and interrupt us to ask if we believed Hauptmann was guilty. One of our photographers would screw flash bulbs in the sockets in the bathroom and when one of the Trenton tramps went in we would hear her scream when she switched on the light and got the full blast of the high-powered bulb right in her eyes. One of our reporters, Sutherland Denlinger, used to sing spirituals and military songs while working. He got so he could sing "Tiddly Winks God Damn" and write an analysis of the previous day's testimony at the same time.

We kept the typewriters going sometimes until 3 A.M., stepping out on the upstairs porch at intervals to watch the snow piling up in the peaceful, deserted village street. In the morning all the ashtrays would be full of butts and the wastebaskets would hold piles of crumpled copy paper and empty applejack bottles. Whenever I see a bottle of applejack I think of the Hauptmann trial. It was a mess. I have seen six men electrocuted, and once a young woman who had been stabbed in the neck died while I was trying to make her lie still, and one night I saw a white-haired Irish cop with a kindly face give a Negro thief the third degree, slowly tearing fresh bandages off wounds in the Negro's back, but for unnecessary inhumanity I do not believe I ever saw anything which surpassed the Hauptmann trial— Mrs. Lindbergh on the witness stand, for example, identifying her murdered child's sleeping suit, or Mrs. Hauptmann the night the jury came in, the night she heard that her husband was to be electrocuted. The older I get the less I care to see such things. I am callous enough to remember, however, that the trial gave me respite from the city room and a lot of country air and country food. It was a mess, but I had fun covering it, and there will never be anything like it again, God willing. That is the way I feel about many of the stories I have worked on.

CHAPTER II

Drunks

1. BAR AND GRILL

Within a few blocks of virtually every large newspaper in the United States except The Christian Science Monitor there is a saloon haunted by reporters, a saloon which also functions as a bank, as a sanitarium, as a gymnasium and sometimes as a home. Dick's Bar and Grill is such a place. It is sometimes possible to see more amazing sights in fifteen minutes in Dick's—especially on a night when Jim Howard, the rewrite man, finds it difficult to roll anything but five aces in one, or on a night when the city editor of the greatest afternoon newspaper in the United States imitates a tree frog, or on a night when Louie, the bartender who likes Chinese food, describes his last square meal at Tingyatsak's, or on a night when Elmer Roessner, the feature editor, gets on all fours to locate a die he has rolled into the fantastic debris behind the bar—than it is in an entire performance of the Ringling Brothers and Barnum & Bailey Circus.

While I never drink anything stronger than Moxie, I often go into Dick's to observe life, a subject in which I have been deeply interested since childhood. This place is down on a narrow street near the Brooklyn Bridge; it is one of those places with a twitchy neon sign, a bar which sags here and there, possibly because it was moved in and out of several speakeasies during prohibition, and a grimy window on which are stuck greasy cardboard signs advertising specials, such as "Special Today. Chicken Pot Pie. Bread & Butter. 35c." There are a big bowl of fresh roasted peanuts and a bottle of mulligan on the bar, and the tile floor is littered with peanut hulls and cigarette ends and bologna rinds from the free lunch. The cook uses olive oil for frying, and he burns a lot of it during the day. On damp days the place smells like a stable, and there is a legend in the neighborhood that truck-drivers in the street outside have to restrain their horses from entering.

The proprietor, Dick, is a sad-eyed and broad-beamed Italian who often shakes his fat, hairy fists at the fly-specked ceiling and screams, "I am being crucified." He hates all his customers, but he is liberal with credit and has a cigar box under the bar full of tabs. If he is feeling good, he slides the bottle toward the customer every third drink and says, "This is on me."

One time Dorothy Hall, a society reporter, took Dick with her to the Beaux Arts Ball. The costumes were supposed to be Oriental, and she got him a eunuch costume. She told him to speak nothing but Italian and introduced him as a big Italian nobleman from Naples. He danced with Elsa Maxwell, who was dressed as a Grand Eunuch.

"She sure did have good manners," he said later.

When he buys a newspaper, he spreads it out on the bar and looks for girls in bathing suits. When he finds one he likes, he says, "My God! Look at this baby. My God! This baby has everything. My God! I would die for her."

The customers hardly ever call him by his name. He is called "The House." For example, a customer will say to a bartender, "Go see if The House will cash a check for me." When he is shaking dice, he always sings. He believes he has a good voice, and his favorite song is "Love in Bloom." When he comes to work, he ties on his apron and looks down the bar at his customers. Then he shakes his head and says, "They must have forgot to lock the doors at the asylum." However, he believes he runs a classy place. He will say with pride, "The last time Mr. Heywood Broun was in here, he said I make the best gin rickey he ever tasted." One time someone stole a sign from one of the chain nut stores, the Chock Full o' Nuts Company, and hung it on his door, and he was angry for days.

The place was once a speakeasy, and twenty minutes after repeal The House had broken all the 1,117 new alcohol regulations. In most of the new saloons, the bartenders reek with the idea of Service and treat the customers with respect, but here the bartenders also hate the customers. This hatred is mutual, and each night the bar is the barrier between two hostile camps. The bartenders do not sympathize with a customer who comes in with a hangover, and they do not prescribe remedies.

"I hope you die," The House often says. "You should leave the state for what you did last night."

There are two steady waiters, and they also hate the customers. One is named Horace. He is an Italian who suffers from adenoids and never shuts his mouth. He has a delusion about his head. He was in the Italian Army during the war, and he believes his head was shot off and that the doctors got the head of an Austrian and sewed it on his neck. He claims that the new head is not satisfactory because it is the head of a young man and often urges him into adventures in which the rest of his body is not particularly interested.

"My other head had a big mustache," he said one night.

The other waiter is a Norwegian named Eddie, whose feet hurt. Fifteen minutes after he is given an order, he comes back and says, "What was it you ordered?" He keeps a bottle of gin on the roof of the icebox and takes a drink every thirty minutes. On Saturday nights, when the rush is over, he puts a raincoat over his waiter's jacket and goes out to look up his enemies. Sometimes after such errands he does not show up for several days, and if a customer inquires, The House says, "He's in Bellevue. I am being crucified."

The cook has a bad temper. One noon a customer came in and looked at the mimeographed menu.

"How is the London broil?" he asked Eddie.

"I'll go see," he said.

In a moment Eddie returned.

"The cook says it's no good," he said.

"Go ask him what is good," commanded the customer.

A few minutes later Eddie came back again.

"The cook says nothing's no good," he said.

Among the customers are four members of a federal inspection service, who are known in the place as "the G-men." When one of them gets a telephone call, he hurries to the booth in the rear and slams the door. This is a signal for the others to rush forward and bang on the wooden sides of the booth with telephone books. One night they tore a booth down. They keep yelling, "Listen to the tom-tom in the jungle." They keep slamming the booth until their enraged colleague rushes out, and then they grab him. They throw him on the floor and sit on him. When he is exhausted and lies still, they take turns talking double-talk into the mouthpiece until the person on the other end hangs up. The fight is repeated three times each night, with a different G-man as the victim each time. The other customers rarely notice the fights any more.

There are two Southerners among the customers. One is from a state which still secedes from the Union at least once every fortnight, and he often talks in a very high-class Southern accent so people will ask him, "Are you from the South?" He is afraid to walk the streets after dark because of Yankees, and always carries a whistle he stole from a drunken policeman. Sometimes on the way home he thinks a Yankee is after him and blows his whistle, summoning police from blocks around. He used to say that corn whiskey was the only whiskey fit to drink and complain bitterly because The House refused to carry it. One night one of the bartenders went up to Harlem and bought a quart, and when the Southerner began complaining about never getting any good old corn whiskey any more, he brought it out. The Southerner felt compelled to buy several drinks of it, and was sick for four days. When The House heard about it, he said, "We always try to please our customers."

The other Southerner is known in the place as Jeeter Lester. He does not like the South, because he could never make a living down there, and now he claims he was born at the northeast corner of Broadway and Forty-second Street. The small, sylvan Southern town in which he was born was so quiet that he takes a psychopathic delight in noise. When he empties a beer glass, he often buys it from the bartender and throws it on the floor. Sometimes the floor around his feet is ankle-deep in broken glass. He was once converted to the Baptist Church by a tent revivalist, and when he is blue he sings hymns. His favorite hymn is "When the Roll Is Called Up Yonder I'll Be There."

"I hope to God you don't favor us with no hymns tonight," The House says when he enters the place.

Jeeter is an expert at snapping a coin, hidden between his fingers, against a highball glass the moment it touches his lips, making a noise as if he had bit a piece out of the glass. Then he screams and spits out a mouthful of ice, which looks a great deal like glass when it is flying through the air. It frightens new customers.

"My God, man," they say, "are you hurt?"

"I am bleeding to death," Jeeter moans, clasping his hand to his mouth and simulating expressions of extreme pain.

There are quite a few women among the regular customers. About once a month a stout bookkeeper for a religious-goods house over on Barclay Street shows up. She used to be a singer in vaudeville. She is a matronly person, and she says she had rickets when she was a child and it left her with a nervous disorder. She has windshield scars running from ear to mouth on both sides of her face, but they do not make her self-conscious. She often points them out to people and says, "I am streamlined." When she is full of beer, she climbs up on the bar and pretends she is sitting on a piano.

"I got ants in my pants," she sings in her lovely soprano voice. "I got a turtle in my girdle."

"I am being crucified," The House screams, pushing her off the bar.

The only man who ever died in this ginmill was a Mr. Friedman. He was extraordinarily fat. He ran a newsstand on West Street and sold newspapers to the New Jersey ferryboat commuters. He was a hard-working man during prohibition, when beer cost a quarter a glass, but when repeal brought the price down to ten cents, he would quit selling papers in the middle of the day and hurry off to Dick's. The night he died was after the day Wiley Post and Will Rogers crashed in Alaska. Everybody who passed the stand bought a paper, and by 3 P.M. he figured he had enough money in his coin apron to finance a night of beer-drinking. Every time Mr. Friedman finished a glass of beer, he would grunt and say, "Well, they can't take that away from me." He often complained about the steaks in the place.

"This steak wasn't hung long enough," he would yell, stabbing the thick air with his fork. "I can't eat this fresh meat. I ain't no cannibal."

In the summer he slept in City Hall Park. Walking across the park to the Third Avenue El, I have often seen him stretched out on a bench, snoring to the moon. The place was full the night he died. He fell off his stool at the bar and began to gasp. The House ran to the booth and called the police. An ambulance doctor examined him while he was stretched out on the tile floor.

"You can hardly call him a man," said the young doctor. "He is just a living barrel of beer."

Just before he died he looked up at the customers gathered around him with drinks in their hands and said, "I drank thirty-two beers tonight." Those were his last words.

"I guess Mr. Friedman is a dead barrel of beer

now," said The House as a committee of customers wrapped up the drunken newsdealer in two table-cloths and carried him out.

An old printer spends whole days and nights in the place, holding to the bar with one hand and making oratorical gestures with the other. He makes a speech which never ends, muttering to himself, and no one knows what he is talking about, except that he is denouncing something.

"What's the matter with him?" new customers ask, staring.

"I never been able to figure out what he's talking about," The House answers. "Hey, Jimmy, tell the man what you're talking about. My God, Jimmy, let us in on the secret."

A cabdriver who was born in England hangs out in the place. His only name is Liverpool. He is probably the only cabdriver in the city doing a credit business. He even sells Irish Sweepstakes tickets on credit. When he is in the place, he makes it his business to answer the telephone. It is practically impossible to reach anybody in the place by telephone. Liverpool will answer a call and yell from the booth, "It's for you, Mr. Kennedy. Are you here?" Mr. Kennedy will shake his head and say, "I ain't here. You haven't seen me since Labor Day." Then you hear Liverpool saying, "No, Miss, he ain't been in since Labor Day."

When Liverpool comes into the place, he looks scornfully at the row of drinkers. He never drinks anything, and when he hauls a drunken customer home on credit he gives him a temperance lecture. Sometimes he has the fare screaming in horror.

"You are a fool to drink," he will yell through the cab window while waiting for a light to change. "You should let it alone. What do you think your liver looks like now? In the morning you will have a bad headache. Now, take me. I don't drink, and I feel fine, just fine. If I didn't have to in the line of business, I would never put my foot in a barroom. My mamma didn't raise no crazy children."

Shaking for drinks by way of a game called Indian Dice is always going on in Dick's. Sometimes as many as fifteen people are shaking in one game, and it costs the man who gets stuck a day's wages to pay the round. The House always shakes. He is a wizard with a dicebox, and sometimes customers drink themselves blind trying to stick him. The game is played with five dice, and no set lasts longer than one night. The losers get mad and throw them into the spittoon just to hear The House scream.

"Listen to him yell," they say. "He got those dice from the five-and-dime, but to hear him yell you would think they was made from precious ivory from the Sudan or someplace."

The House does not have any trouble with police-

men. He knows them all. One rainy night a policeman came in and got drunk. Then he took out his
revolver and began to have target practice, using the
telephone booth for a target. The House sidled out of
the place and telephoned the police station, and two
other policemen came and took the marksman away.
The House keeps a bottle under the bar for them and
calls it "the cops' bottle." This bottle contains a blend
of Scotch and rye, made up of drinks left unfinished
by paying customers. One big cop always snorts
when he has his drink and says, "This must be some
of that new kind of whiskey which they distill from
axle grease."

There used to be a pin game in the place which
paid off beginning at a score of 13,500, but one night
the customer called Jeeter Lester got a screwdriver
and fixed up some bolts on the machine. He fixed it
so you got at least 30,000, even if you shot wild, and
everybody who played it collected at least a quarter
before The House found out why there were so many
expert pin-game players among his customers and
called the company to take the damned thing out of
his place.

A lot of fights start in Dick's Bar and Grill, but
they do not end there. There is a vacant loft upstairs,
and when customers begin taking pokes at one another, The House makes them go up there and fight
it out. One of the bartenders will help them up the

stairs, and soon the sound of scuffling and swearing will reach the customers below. Once a man was knocked out on a Friday night, and his opponent came downstairs and continued his drinking. Sunday morning the bartender went upstairs for something and found the loser on the floor, still asleep. When he was aroused and told about the passage of time, he took it all right.

"I needed sleep anyway," he said.

2. The Year of Our Lord 1936, or Hit Me, William

Saloonkeepers are extremely useful to reporters in New York City. The dreary business of locating people takes up most of a reporter's time, and in many neighborhoods, especially in tenement neighborhoods, the saloonkeeper is apt to know the address or hangout of any citizen dopey enough or unlucky enough to be of interest to a great metropolitan newspaper. When a person suddenly gets into the news—a happy idiot who wins an Irish Sweepstakes prize, for instance, or a woman who murders her sweetheart because she loves him so—the reporter is frequently able to piece together an accurate picture of the person by talking with the saloonkeeper, the delicatessen proprietor, the undertaker (half the people in any poor neighborhood owe money to the undertaker), and the grocer. In any neighborhood these gentlemen know all the gossip, and unlike the priest, who also knows all the gossip, they do not mind talking, giving you the worst they know. Of these, however, the saloonkeeper is usually the best informed.

The saloonkeeper is also useful because he can be interviewed about anything. This is an example: If a war breaks out anywhere in the world an idea for a local story always takes form in the frenzied brain of the feature editor, and the idea is always the same. If the war is between Italy and Ethiopia, for instance, the idea is, "How do the Italians in New York City feel about the war?" When a reporter is assigned to such a story he goes on a hurried tour of the ginmills in the nearest Italian neighborhood (Mulberry Street if he works for The World-Telegram and Harlem's Little Italy if he works for The Herald Tribune) and in his story each saloonkeeper is identified as "a community leader."

When I am assigned to interview an "authority" on anything I sometimes find it wise to head for the nearest saloon and interview the bartender. One bitter afternoon in December 1936, I was told to find "an authority on mass insanity" and ask him to review the insane happenings of 1936. The best authority on mass insanity I could think of was Gilligan F. Holton, an eccentric Negro saloonkeeper and gambler, who ran the Broken Leg and Busted Bar & Grill in a basement on West 138th Street until the end of 1931 when the cops tore the door down and put him in jail for seven months because he could not keep order among the society matrons who frequented the establishment.

I located Mr. Holton in a bar and grill operated by one of his former bartenders, a corner bar and grill on Third Avenue. He said he was completing a dissertation in which he expected to prove that William Shakespeare was a Moor, a dissertation he began years ago while working as a servant for David Belasco, but that he was willing to knock off work for a few hours and give me a discourse on certain examples of mass insanity in 1936. Before he began the discourse he ordered a beer. The bartender pushed the glass across the bar. Mr. Holton picked it up and called for a soup spoon. Holding the spoon daintily, with his little finger outstretched, he scooped the foam off the top of the beer.

"I never could stand whipped cream," he said. "It don't agree with me."

When he had removed the collar from his beer Mr. Holton drank it with one triumphant gulp. Then he looked scornfully at the bartender and said, "Put it on my tab, you bum."

Then he sat down at a table.

"It sure was a nutty year," he said, gazing into the distance like a seer. "More high-class nuts running around than you would think the world would hold. There was times when I thought the whole damned population had gone off and ate themselves a bait of loco weed. Each time some new thing came up my wife, Mrs. Ida, would try it out on me. Like one night she woke me up and said, 'Knock, knock.' I knew she was trying to get me to say, 'Who's there?' But I just said, 'Shut up, Mrs. Ida.' She kept on knock-knocking, and I picked up an automobile jack I keep handy beside the bed and hit her over the head with it.

"The next night she came in and began to wiggle her fingers and stick out her tongue. I said to her, 'What's the matter this time, Mrs. Ida?' She said, 'What's this?' She kept on wiggling her fingers and I just looked at her. Then she said, 'Don't you catch on? I am imitating a cash register.' I picked up my automobile jack and let her have it right where it would do the most good. I am too old for that sort of by-play. I reached my majority years and years ago. I do not wear long pants just because they become me."

Mr. Holton sighed and shook his head. He said things got so bad at home that he wrote Santa Claus and asked him to give Mrs. Ida "a new set of brains." He said he believed the song "The Music Goes 'Round and 'Round" had an effect on his mind which would last for many years.

"There was a time when I thought the dogcatcher

would come for me at any moment," he said. "I could just see myself up at the State asylum, the star freshman at the State asylum."

He began to bang on the table and the bartender rushed forward with a beer and a soup spoon. However, Mr. Holton disregarded the beer. He jumped up and began to scamper about the tiled floor of the bar and grill.

"You push the middle valve down," he yelled. "Boom, boom."

He jumped up and down as he sang.

"The music goes 'round and 'round," he yelled. "Boom, boom."

He ran over to the bartender and said, "Hit me, William, hit me."

The bartender hit him over the head with a chair. Then Mr. Holton smiled happily.

"I feel better now," he said, sitting down and drinking his beer.

He said that during the forthcoming year he hoped to establish himself as a cult leader.

"Sort of on the order of Father Divine, but more refined," he said. "Now, there's a man who contributed a lot to 1936. I won't say what he contributed, but he sure did contribute. My cult will be a thing of beauty. I'm going to get a lot of doll-babies gathered around me, the fattest bunch of women I can find. I like fat women. I'm going to teach them to yell,

'Thank you, Father,' every time I draw in my breath. On second thought I think I'll teach them to say, 'Thank you, Papa.' That will improve on Father Divine.

"Also, I will make all the people in my cult talk in the unknown tongue. It is so cute. I would have joined up with Father Divine's movement myself, except I found out that there is no beer in the icebox up in his Promised Land. Plenty of spare-ribs, but no beer."

He said that 1936 was indeed a screwy year, but that 1931 beat all the years he ever saw.

"I was running my Broken Leg and Busted Bar & Grill full blast that year," he said. "It was one of those 'intimate' places. The people would stand for anything that year. One night the place was crowded, and a man and his wife came in. He looked like a big spender. I decided to use him for a psychological test, a test to determine just how much a human being will stand for.

"I sat him at a table right near the kitchen where it was so warm it would singe your hair. Then I had the waiters spill soup on him and step on his feet and scrape crumbs into his lap. His wife ordered some wine, and I said to myself, 'I'll fix her.' I got me some cold tea and I poured some kerosene in it and I dumped a little gin in it and I shook it up. Well, this couple stayed in the place until daybreak and spent

$125—which was easy to do, of course—and then the man came up to me. I thought he was going to hit me.

"But no. He said, 'Mr. Holton, I want to thank you for a wonderful night. I never had such an interesting time. I am going to tell all my friends about your place.'

"And then his wife said, 'And the wine, Mr. Holton! How marvelous! The most wonderful Amontillado sherry I ever tasted. How do you get such wonderful wine in this beastly prohibition country?'

"After that I gave up."

Mr. Holton talked for two hours and in the middle of the second hour he became incoherent. Finally he stretched out in a booth in the back room of the bar and grill and went to sleep. I left him there, snoring happily, and went back to my office and wrote the story on mass insanity. My city editor approved the story and said that Mr. Holton should be elected President of the Psychiatric Association of America. About six months later I went up to Harlem to ask Mr. Holton to help me locate one of the heads of the numbers lottery for an interview. He wasn't in the pool room on Lenox Avenue in which I sometimes found him, nor was he in the fried-fish café operated by one of his fat women friends. I couldn't find him anywhere. A few days later I was walking by the café and the woman came out on the sidewalk and said she heard I had been inquiring after Mr. Holton. She said, "I just wanted to let you know that he kicked the bucket in Bellevue." Mr. Holton died insane. His disease was general paresis.

God rest his soul.

CHAPTER III

Cheese-Cake

1. Some Virgins, No Professionals

If you smirk enough you can get away with practically anything in a New York newspaper and once it is understood that Sex is to be treated coyly or as melodrama, one of the most amusing classes of people to interview are naked people—nudists, strip tease girls, models, dancers who believe that to be artistic you just start unbuttoning. Such people abound in New York City, a city whose women are remarkably narcissistic, and in the last five or six years I have seen interviews with them become part of the feature writer's routine.

Such interviews are known as "cheese-cake," a term originally used by photographers for any shot in which a female has been induced to assume a sexy pose but more specifically for those standardized photographs taken on decks of liners in which a girl poses with her dress lifted above her knees. Handing a ship-news assignment to a photographer, a picture editor will say, "See if you can pick up some cheese-cake on this boat." (I do not know the origin of the term. Except for "cheese-cake" and "lobster-shift," most newspaper slang is explicable and off-hand, such as "hot squat" for an electrocution and "dry dive" for an out-the-window suicide and "slug" for the identification words—SLAY for a murder; SNATCH for a kidnaping—on sheets of copy.) There is one newspaper in New York City which prints acres of cheese-cake, but you should see one of their holy, down-with-it editorials about burlesque; in my opinion a pimp is a cherub compared with the two-faced editorial writer of this newspaper.

The classic example of cheese-cake is a series of photographs of a French dancer made in her stateroom on the Ile de France. She did not understand any English at all and when the assembled photographers made gestures indicating that she should lift her dress a little so her celebrated legs would show in the picture she misunderstood and cheerfully lifted her dress up to her neck. Photographers exchange cheese-cake, and the utterly candid photographs of the French dancer hang in newspaper darkrooms all over the United States.

Much typewritten cheese-cake is about strip-tease girls. The feature writer is responsible, as a matter of fact, for the current popularity of burlesque in a dozen cities. He is, however, not always welcome backstage in New York houses, managers knowing that when newspapers run an unusual number of stories about strippers the reformers throw catfits and in a short time the industry has to be, as Variety terms it, Sapolioed.

I am not opposed to cheese-cake stories on principle. They mirror a form of life which pullulates in this city, and a few of them are funny. The ads I see every morning in the subway—the constipation cure ads, for instance, especially those of the chocolate-covered ones—are far more disgusting to me than anything I have ever seen or heard in a burlesque house. There is little variety in cheese-cake, however, and the fact that there has to be a smirk or an ogle in every paragraph sometimes makes it unpleasant reading. I think there is too much of it. I think, as a matter of fact, that burlesque strippers are a great deal like elephants; when you've seen one you've seen them all. I think I found out all I will ever want to know about burlesque in one afternoon. I will tell about this afternoon.

The house was the Apollo and it is on West Forty-second Street. When I arrived the second show of the day, the 3:30, was moving along and the first stripper, copper-haired Margie Hart, was taking off her clothes out on the horseshoe stage. Backstage a mob of naked young women were standing around, yawning, waiting to pony-prance out on the stage with grins on their tired faces. The flyman stood with one hand tightened on a rope, ready to snatch a drop into the air for the comedy bit which customarily follows the first stripper. There were thirty-eight girls in the show and backstage everything was crowded.

The show was a little behind time and Miss Hart, who is well-set-up, was working fast. She didn't "work up." Just before the third blackout she let out a yell, slipped out of her filmy, pink step-ins and tossed them into the wings. Except for her G-string, a pair of blue shoes, the rouge on her lovely cheeks and the fillings in her teeth, she was naked as the day she was born. She gave the customers a couple of grinds and a series of hot bumps and her strip was over. Although the customers—"the boys"—kept smacking their hands together insistently, she was seen no more, the sweet thing.

A moment later a stuttering comedian began one of burlesque's basic comedy scenes, the scene in the doctor's office, a scene with a multitude of variations. (Each comic has his own variation of the court scene, the honeymoon scene, the night-clerk scene, the cop in the alley scene, etc., and he can play them "slow" or "dirty," according to how the censors feel at the moment.) The straight, or talking-woman, waited in the wings until it was time for her to strut out with her hands on her lean hips. She rested against a boomerang, a stanchion for a wing flood-light. Lifting one of her bare legs, she scratched an ankle. Her eyes were sleepy.

In a minute she was on the stage, wide-awake, and backstage you could hear her talking, telling the doc she sure did need about two dollars worth of his best advice. Then there was the report of a loud slap in the face. They talked fast and only at intervals could the lines be distinguished backstage. You could hear her jumping up and down and chanting, "Oh, doctor, I feel so good. Oh, doctor, I feel so good." You could hear the stuttering doc get off some gag about mercy-killing. He jumped up and down as he talked.

The reason for this insane leaping about is obscure. Sometimes comics will forget all about the bit in which they are working and start jumping up and down, chanting some unrelated line, such as "Meet you around the corner in a half an hour. Meet you around the corner in a half an hour."

After the climax gag and the blackout, a "number girl," a singer who leads numbers, strolled out on the stage singing "These Foolish Things (Remind Me of You)." The number girl was Mary Joyce, a nice blonde with a nice voice, and when she knocked off, the curtains opened and the stage was crowded with girls. The chorus danced out toward the customers and then danced back in, gently bobbing the transparent bibs over their breasts. The haughty showgirls paraded. Then the toe-line, a chorus of ballet girls from the Fokine school, an innovation in burlesque, tiptoed out.

"Let's catch this toe number," said Emmett Callahan, managing director of the Apollo, who was backstage for a few minutes.

He got out of his chair beneath the call board, and pushed his way into the wings. The pert little girls in the ballet tiptoed this way and that. They made a sudden dip in unison and their short, starched skirts billowed out. Mr. Callahan watched them with approval, smiling at the leader as she danced into the wings.

Mr. Callahan is one of burlesque's bright boys. He came from Toledo, where Joe E. Brown was in his class in public school. He used to work in vaudeville— "Midgie Miller & The Callahan Brothers." He has been in the show business twenty-six years, mostly around New York, and now, even including the Minskys, he is probably the most important burlesque impresario.

He is the husband of Ann Corio, by far the most popular stripper, the girl who once drew down $1,900 for a week in Cleveland, topping Gypsy Rose Lee by hundreds and hundreds of dollars. She works on a percentage basis, taking a big cut of the profits. Mr. Callahan calls her "Annie."

"Classy little shrimps," said Mr. Callahan, survey-ing his ballet.

When the ballet finished up, three Negro tap-dancers in fancy brown tuxedos clattered out. Mr. Callahan, uninterested, left the wings and went back to his chair. Unclothed girls stood all around him, but he did not notice them. When one girl passed he nodded when she spoke, and said, "How's your cough, Mary?" The little girl said, "Oh, I'm O.K., Mr. Callahan."

A cough is unusual in a burlesque company, and colds are practically unknown. The hardihood of the overworked and underpaid burlesque girls is amaz-ing. They work naked, sometimes in drafty houses, and they make quick changes in overheated dressing rooms and then run down cold stairways, but they are rarely under the weather. Mr. Callahan said the exercise they get makes them robust; stomping their way through four or five shows a day the girls get more exercise than a fighter in a training camp.

The conduct of the girls backstage is always dis-appointing to reformers. Out on the stage they will work naked and feel no embarrassment, but when they run backstage and climb the stairs to their dress-ing rooms they try to cover themselves up.

Conversation between the girls and the men in the stage crew is forbidden. The boyfriends of the girls are not allowed to come backstage. As a matter of fact, it is hard for any outsider to get permission to go backstage in a burlesque theater in this city. The days when Billy Minsky used to permit gents from the Racquet and Tennis Club to stand in the wings are gone with Billy.

Each chorus has a captain, a girl with a sense of responsibility, who can impose fines on her colleagues if, for example, she catches them chewing gum on the stage. If a girl sits down on a dusty backstage bench, getting her costume dirty, the chorus captain says, "Stand up." If the girls chatter too loud in the wings the captain says, "Dry up, kids." In the business the girls are always referred to as "the kids."

If they show up tipsy, they are tossed out of the show. Even a beer breath warrants a bawling out. Burlesque, of course, is a target for all sorts of reformers. If men were allowed to congregate at the stage door, as they congregate at the stage doors of the $5.50 musical comedies, or if a girl were drunk on the stage, the Women's League Against Everything would be in the manager's hair in a few hours.

The crusades carried on by sin-haters and license commissioners have given people a low opinion of the character of the burlesque girl, an opinion at variance with the facts. The girls work too hard for tabloid orgies. A girl who has jumped up and down a stage for twelve or fourteen hours a day does not want an orgy; all she wants is a quiet place to sleep.

When a burlesque producer is asked in court about the morals of his workers, the answer always is, "Some virgins, no professionals." You would probably find that the private lives of any twenty stenographers who work in Wall Street and live in Greenwich Village are more lurid than the private lives of a similar number of burlesque girls. You would undoubtedly find that the kids at the Apollo would be shocked by the private lives of some society girls.

"Working in burlesque isn't so awful for a girl," said Miss Lilly Berg, an elegant showgirl who doesn't have to grind and bump like the chorus. "I used to work in one of the biggest department stores in this city, and I prefer this. I make more dough, and I'm not so exhausted at night. You can't even sit down in a department store. It's also better than working in a cabaret or a dance hall. The customers here are so far away you can't smell the garlic. In a store a cranky old woman can come in and get fresh, and you have to stand there and take it. But if a customer gets fresh here he gets a sock on the puss."

The burlesque producer looks upon the censor as one of the persistent evils of his business, like damage suits and comedians who show up drunk. No person in the world can grow as angry as a producer who opens his newspaper and sees the headline "Burlesque Told to End Obscenity; Commissioner Gives Houses One Day to Clean Up Shows or Lose Their Licenses." The producer feels that he is being made the goat, and he shouts that his girls wear as much as the girls in the expensive cabarets.

He knows that the comedy on his stage is about as low as comedy can be, but he says Dwight Fiske sings about the same things at the Savoy Plaza, and the cops don't try to pull him away from his piano, do they? He shouts that the poor man is entitled to his depravity as well as the rich. He feels that he is being persecuted, and most of the time his feelings are justified.

He says the strip act is a work of art. He says a citizen ought to realize that a burlesque show is not Sunday school and abstain from buying tickets if it shocks him.

"We don't compel the customers to buy tickets," said Mr. Callahan. "This is a free country. I'd like to run burlesque as a cheap revue, but I'm in Rome and I got to be a Roman. I can't go Presbyterian when every burlesque show and every night club in town is working naked."

The burlesque girl sweats for her money.

"The kids in the chorus pull down $25.70 a week, including extra compensation for the Saturday midnight," said Mr. Callahan. "On the road it runs to $28.30 for the girls in the line, and the same for showgirls. That's the minimum. We've paid showgirls as high as $32.50. A straight woman gets $75. The strippers are the backbone of the show, and most of them get paid from $60 to $125. That is, the large majority of strippers range between these figures, but some get paid a lot more. A few work for a percentage of the profits. A good salary for a stripper in this city is $125. Margie Hart is a $125 girl. Sometimes the girls get paid more out of town."

There are three general styles of stripping—"fast," "hot," and "sweet."

Miss Corio works sweet and slow. She wears a lot more than most strippers when she begins and when she ends, and she is more feminine than tigerish in her strut across the stage. She is not addicted to the bump, a movement in which the knees are bent and the hips are thrown backward and forward with, in some girls, an almost startling rapidity. Nor is she expert with the grind, which is, of course, a rotary motion of the hips something like the hootchy-kootchy. All burlesque girls must know how to bump and grind. Except for the minstrel show, the strip act is probably America's only original contribution to the theater, and the bump and grind are integral parts of the orthodox strip.

Most strippers have some little trick or other, a

wriggle or a distinctive manner of loosening shoulder straps, which distinguishes them from their colleagues. Carrie Finnell, a fat girl, has a comedy strip in which she does what she calls "a control dance." Unfortunately, it cannot be described here. Evelyn Myers, another headliner, has an unusual wriggle; only a snake could copy it.

Peaches Strange is celebrated for blending the shimmy with the strip. Gypsy Rose Lee, like Ann Corio, is fond of working with a lot of clothes. At the Irving Place, she used to come out dressed in a big white fur coat, a coat with a lot of buttons on it. She would glide languidly across the stage, a sort of bound-for-the-opera walk. On her way back into the wings she would twitch the coat open with a negligent gesture, and the customers would go crazy, the bums.

The most dynamic of the strippers is Georgia Sothern, who has the kind of red hair usually described as "flaming." Miss Sothern works hot. She bounds across a stage, flinging her red head up and down, bumping, grinding. Sometimes at a wild Saturday midnight she will go through all the chorus-girl routines in one strip—the Texas Tommy, the fly-away, walking the dog, the toe punch, falling off a log. All the time she will be taking off her filmy clothes and putting them back on again. She will even do all the kicks if she is feeling good, the muscle kick, the hitch kick and the fan kick. Between the kicks she will shout, "Let's go, boys." After a blackout on a Sothern strip the customers fall back into their seats, exhausted.

"She's going to drop dead on the stage one of these nights," said Mr. Callahan. "She's got too much fire in her for her own good. She strips like she just had dynamite for lunch."

The burlesque girl is proud of her tricks. A girl who can accomplish an unusual grind is respected. Dressing-room conversation is largely shop talk although they gab a lot about men and clothes, like all women. If Margie Hart comes out with a new way of wearing her red hair the kids will crowd into the wings, whispering, "Look at Margie's hair. Do you like it that way? She's a fool to change."

The girls hang out together; they are overworked and underpaid, but they like the life and they are companions in misery. In this respect they resemble nurses and newspaper reporters. They frequent the same restaurants. If they don't have boyfriends waiting to buy their dinners, a mob of them goes to the same restaurant or delicatessen. Just before the finale on the 3:30 show they begin talking about where they will eat.

"Where you going to eat?" one will yell.

"Anywhere but the fish place. I'm sick of that joint."

"Let's go to the chow mein place tonight."

"Okie doke, baby. Hey, Woodsy, you wanna get some chow mein?"

At the restaurant they talk about the business. If a comedian stuck a new line into his bit during the last show they appraise it. For example, if the comic judge in the court scene says "We got to take this to a higher court" and puts his chair on the bench and sits up there during the rest of the scene, the girls decide whether it is O.K. or lousy. What they really love, however, is a comedian who makes cracks about a rival burlesque house during a show. Most of these cracks have to do with the antiquity of the girls in the other show.

"Geeze," said one the other night, over her bowl of chicken chow mein, "Joey Fay got off a good one last week in Philly. He took Rosemary out to the lights and he introduced her. He said, 'I want all you nice people to give this little girl a big hand because her mother just had a terrible accident. Her mother just fell off the running board over at the Star and Garter.' "

A "running board" is the runway extending out into the audience on which the chorus prances. They are not permitted in New York City any more.

The Women's League Against Everything thinks they are awful.

2. NUDE, DEFINITELY NUDE

When anything gets as popular as the strip-tease act someone always comes along and tries to do the reverse of it. One morning Mr. Samuel J. Burger telephoned my office that he had just begun to manage "a Chicago dame, and my God, she's so unusual she's got me nuts." I did not feel well that morning, so I was sent up to interview her. Mr. Burger is a thin, inspired, wax-mustached Broadway promoter who books for vaudeville such spectacles as the juries of murder trials, the relatives of murdered criminals, bubble dancers and Indian mind readers.

His latest attraction turned out to be a shy young woman with a business school education, a giggle and a pair of hosiery-ad gams. She was nineteen years old and her name was Jan Marsh. We met her in a theatrical hotel, and she demonstrated her act.

"I may be nuts." she said, slipping out of her dress, "but I think I have an act which will ruin the strip-tease racket."

She tossed her dress on the arm of a chair, and then she took off her shoes and stockings. Then she took off an assortment of black lace undergarments.

"Now look," she said, unnecessarily. "This is the way I start my act. I begin where the strip-tease ends. I am nude, definitely nude. Oh, definitely. I come out in front of the audience in that condition. I slip

on my black lace panties. Then I put on a garter belt.
Then I slip on my black net stockings. Black is such a
fascinating color. Then I get into my shoes. Then I get
into my dress, a zipper dress, the kind of dress they
call a taxicab dress. Then I pin on a corsage of flowers, orchids maybe. Then I put on my coat and hat.
Then I put on another coat, maybe two or three
coats. I just keep on getting into clothes until the
audience begins to moan. I put on maybe a ton of
clothes. I may be nuts, definitely nuts, but I think my
act will ruin the strip-tease racket, which I think
would be a great service to my country."

Miss Marsh grinned. Then she executed a few
dance steps.

"Of course," she said, "when I begin the act I am
as nude as any tease stripper. Definitely."

"She does it all for art," said Mr. Burger.

"That is right," said Miss Marsh. "I do it for art
and I don't mean I have a boy friend by the name of
Art. I have seen the enormous success of these vo-
luptuous strip-tease women, but I do not think the
public is really interested in that kind of thing. I am
a sweet, natural girl. I am not like those bouncy
women. I think that when I do the reverse of the
strip-tease it will be enormously popular and will
start a new movement. I don't smoke or drink. Of
course, if I liked the way it tasted I would, but I think
whiskey is horrible. I am a good swimmer. I am just

a natural American girl, and I think the public would prefer that to one of those bouncy women."

Miss Marsh said she was born in South Amboy, New Jersey, but that the family moved to Chicago when she was a child. Her mother and her father are divorced. She said her mother knows that she came to New York City to ruin the strip-tease racket and does not mind. She said she went to Chicago High School, then to Drake's Business College. Then she got a job as a secretary to a woman who worked for the city.

"She was in the tax department, or something," said Miss Marsh.

The young woman said that when she was younger she used to pose for artists.

"I like to pose for artists," she said. "They are so serious. You stand in front of them nude for hours, but they do not take any interest in you except from an artistic standpoint, which I like. You are just an inspiration to them. I am not a wild girl. I do not even approve of necking."

Miss Marsh smiled.

"She is the society type," said Mr. Burger.

"Yes," said Miss Marsh.

She said that recently she saved up some money and decided to come to New York City and go on the stage.

"I had this idea about reversing the strip-tease,"

she said, "and people told me I was crazy. Then I heard about Mr. Burger, and I decided he must have the same kind of mind I have. I went to see him and I found he had."

"Great minds run in the same channel," said Mr. Burger, flicking some cigarette ashes out of the white carnation in the lapel of his overcoat.

3 . TANYA

At one time or another I have talked with several of the lovely young women who hope to become the Sally Rand of the New York World's Fair of 1939 and I know how ambitious they are. I hope none of them felt thwarted when they read that Mr. Grover A. Whalen had decided to ban "all amusements of the fan-dance type" from the Fair's 280-acre Midway. I hope they will pay no attention to Mr. Whalen and will keep right on trying to invent a new dance, something to take the place of those exposition favorites—the muscle dance, the hootchy-kootchy, the fan dance, the butterfly dance, the bubble or balloon dance, and the swan dance, all of which are rather old-fashioned now.

Mr. Whalen is president of the New York World's Fair Corporation and it is only natural that he should want to ban such artistry, but it surprised me when he took the bit in his teeth and also banned that good sound American word "Midway." He appears to prefer the pompous phrase "Amusement Area." Speaking about the carnival section of the Fair, Mr. Whalen said, "It has been definitely decided not to call it a "Midway." The word seems to have a connotation of evil to Mr. Whalen, although every state and county fair, and nearly every amusement park, has a Midway and the word is recognized in the dictionaries. I don't believe Mr. Whalen's ban on "amusements of the fan-dance type" will be enforced; in fact, I believe the Flushing Meadows will practically crawl with nude wrigglers of one sort or another in 1939. I also believe that most visitors to the Fair will call the carnival section the Midway; the headline-writers on the newspapers will see to that.

Mr. Whalen's outburst of euphemism is unusual, but his decision to ban wriggle dancers is not. The making of this decision is one of the routine duties of exposition executives. Mr. Rufus C. Dawes made the decision when the Century of Progress Exposition was being planned in Chicago in 1929. Mr. Dawes was the president, and he said, "No entertainment of the Little Egypt type will be permitted at the Exposition." Mr. Dawes is probably sitting somewhere at this moment staring at a ceiling and mumbling those words over to himself, dully; by the time his Exposition was dismantled, Sally Rand was a national figure, and there still are millions of Americans who have never even heard of Mr. Rufus C. Dawes.

Mr. Whalen practically duplicated the Dawes decision. He said, "No entertainment of the Sally Rand type will be permitted at the Fair." After the Fair gets under way, Mr. Whalen will certainly be surprised when the newspapers start paying more attention to the inevitable nude wriggler than they do to him, or even to George Washington, whose inaugural as the first President of the United States the Fair is supposed to commemorate. Mr. Whalen is an idealist and he thinks his trylon and his perisphere are more important than sideshows. He can't be blamed for hoping that visitors will be less interested in the Midway dancers than in such educational exhibits as "The Arts and the Basic Industries." Exactly the reverse of this, however, has been the traditional fate of American expositions, and there is no reason the New York World's Fair of 1939 should escape.

I don't really believe many people will take Mr. Whalen seriously. I know a girl who is all prepared to become the Sally Rand of the Fair, and if she read about his ban, I am sure it made her giggle. Of the several girls, similarly prepared, whom I have talked to, she is my favorite. Her name is Florence Cubitt, and she was the Queen of the Nudists at the California Pacific International Exposition at San Diego in 1936. The nudists—twenty girls and five bearded men—were segregated behind a fence in a big field, and the customers paid forty cents to go in and watch from a distance while they played games. Her Exposition name was Tanya Cubitt, she told me, because "Tanya sounds more sexy than Florence." I met her on St. Patrick's Day in 1936, and I spent several hours of a rainy afternoon listening to her talk in her room at the Hotel New Yorker.

Miss Cubitt was sent here to get some publicity for the San Diego Exposition. It is this fact, as much as any other, that makes me think Mr. Whalen's stern statement would cause her to giggle. The officials of the San Diego fair, which was supposed to "tell the story of mankind's restless urge toward achievement," also said they would ban "all but the highest type of concession," but when customers stayed away by the million, they decided that Miss Cubitt's nudist concession was of an extraordinarily high type. More than one American exposition has been saved from bankruptcy by uninhibited young women.

The newspaper for which I work sent me up to interview Miss Cubitt the day after she arrived in New York. A photographer went along with me. I saved all my notes, and I want to tell you about Miss Cubitt because I think she will be one of the sensations of the Midway at Mr. Whalen's Fair.

We were met at the door of Miss Cubitt's room by one of the Exposition's press agents, a brisk young man named Jack Adams. We went in and sat down, and he said the Queen—he called her the Queen every time he referred to her—would be out in a minute. I had a bad cold that day and did not particularly like the assignment. I liked it even less when Mr. Adams began telling me about the Queen. He said she did not approve of the girls in the New York night-club shows because she felt they besmirched the cause of nudism. He said she ate uncooked carrots, took an orange-juice bath about once a week and lived almost entirely off raw herbs.

He was telling about the Queen's dietary habits when she came in. She was naked. It was the first time a woman I had been sent to interview ever came into the room naked, and I was shocked. I say she was naked. Actually, she had a blue G-string on, but I have never seen anything look so naked in my life as she did when she walked into that room. She didn't even have any shoes on. She was a tall girl with a cheerful baby face. She had long golden hair and hazel eyes. The photographer was bending over his camera case, screwing a bulb into his flashpan, when she came in. As soon as he saw her, he abruptly stood erect.

"My God!" he said.

Mr. Adams introduced the Queen, and she shook hands with me and smiled. Then she shook hands with the photographer.

"Pleased to meet you," said the photographer.

"Likewise," said Miss Cubitt, smiling.

She went over and sat down in one of the hotel's overstuffed chairs and said she hoped we wouldn't mind if she didn't put anything on, and we shook our heads in unison. The telephone rang and Mr. Adams answered it. When he got through with the telephone, he said he would have to beat it, that he had an appointment with an advertising agency, and he said goodbye. The rain was beating against the windows, and when Mr. Adams got to the door, Miss Cubitt yelled, "You better wear your rubbers." The photographer was still standing in the middle of the floor with his flashpan in his hand, staring openmouthed at the young woman. I didn't know how to begin the interview.

"Well, Miss Cubitt," I said, tentatively, "Mr. Adams just told me you eat a lot of raw carrots."

"Why," she said, sitting upright in the overstuffed chair, "I never ate a raw carrot in my life. I eat like anybody else. My mother cooks me great big old steaks and French-fried potatoes. That's what I eat. In the nudist colony, the men nudists eat a lot of that stuff. The men nudists are a bunch of nuts. Why, they eat peas right out of the pod. They squeeze the juice out of vegetables and drink it, and they don't eat salt. Also, they have long beards. They don't have any ambition. They just want to be nudists all their lives.

I want to be a dancer, myself. I'm going to come to the New York World's Fair with my dance, and I bet it will make me a reputation."

I saw that the young woman was articulate, and that I wouldn't have to ask a lot of questions. When I said I had a bad cold, she said, "You poor man," and telephoned room service to send up whiskey. At the same time she ordered some sandwiches, some corned-beef sandwiches, saying, "I'm so hungry I could eat the flowers off the plate." While she was holding the telephone in her hand, waiting for room service to answer, she said she was only nineteen years old and that she had eight sisters, four of whom had been working with her in the nudist colony. Their names, she told me, were Ruthie, Bobbie, Lucille and Diane. She said her mother was glad they were working in the colony.

"It keeps us out in the open," said Miss Cubitt. "It doesn't keep us out late at night, and we have a healthy atmosphere to work in. My girl friends think we have orgies and all, but I never had an orgy yet. Sometimes when the sun is hot, nudism is hard work."

She was a pretty girl. Her skin was ivory-colored and she had freckles on her cheeks, like Myrna Loy. In fact, she looked a little like Myrna Loy. She was obviously healthy, and she said she played a lot of tennis and handball. She said she sometimes posed for artists. "Once one of them told me I looked like a Madonna," she said, "and I said, 'O.K.' " I think she was the least inhibited person I ever saw. She reminded me of Reri, the Polynesian girl Florenz Ziegfeld brought to New York in 1931. Reri's feet were always dirty, because she insisted on walking about the theater barefooted, and she used to sit in her dressing room at the "Follies" reading a movie magazine and wearing nothing but a pair of men's trunks.

"Mr. Adams told me you don't approve of the dancers in night clubs here," I said when she sat down again, "because you feel they besmirch the cause of nudism."

Miss Cubitt giggled.

"Well," she said, "you can put that in the paper if you want to, but I went to a night club last night and I thought the girls were real sweet. I would like to get a job in one. I sure do like New York. I've had lobsters every meal since I got here, and last night I had some real French champagne."

After the photographer had been introduced to the Queen, he had slumped into a chair and had remained there, staring. Now he roused himself and said he wanted to make some shots in a hurry, because he had to leave and cover the St. Patrick's Day parade. The young woman enjoyed posing and seemed to be sorry when the photographer finished, although he made about five times as many pictures as we needed. A few minutes after he left, a waiter, bringing the whiskey and the corned-beef sandwiches, knocked on the door. The waiter was either extremely sophisticated or had waited on the Queen before, because he did not seem to notice that she was not wearing anything. His eyes were respectfully averted, but he acted as if all the young women he waited on were nudists. When he had arranged his plates and glasses on a table, he handed Miss Cubitt the check. She signed it, and he bowed and left.

While we were eating the sandwiches, she told me of the dance she was working on, saying she called it the Tiger Lily dance. Why she called it that was a secret, she said.

"A World's Fair," the Queen remarked, "is a good place for a girl to make a reputation. When you get a reputation, you are fixed. Look at Sally Rand. What's she got I haven't got? I've seen her, and she's no world-beater. Look at Rosita Royce and her butterfly dance. Look at Toto La Verne and her swan dance. They're all World's Fair girls. If I can put my Tiger Lily over at the World's Fair, I'll be fixed."

I warned her that she might live to regret a World's Fair reputation, and mentioned the career of Mrs. Frieda Spyropolous, the Syrian girl whose dance as Little Egypt at the World's Columbian Exposition in 1893 attracted more attention than the seventy-ton telescope or any of the other educational exhibits. I told her how this Little Egypt had married the respectable Mr. Andrew Spyropolous, a Greek restaurant proprietor, not long after the Columbian Exposition closed, expecting to settle down to a peaceful way of life, and how the scandalous behavior of the hundreds of other Little Egypts who began doing her dance in low places all over the country had caused her acute anguish the rest of her life.

"Oh, I won't regret it," said the Queen, chewing on her sandwich. "I won't do anything unless it's artistic. Why, out at San Diego they even wanted me to do a Lady Godiva on a big white horse. I didn't do it because my boy friend made me mad. He said to go ahead and be Lady Godiva. He said he would sure pay forty cents to see me do it, because it had been years and years since he'd seen a horse."

Miss Cubitt giggled.

After we finished the sandwiches, we sat at a window and looked at the drizzle. I pointed out a few skyscrapers, but they didn't interest her. She wanted to talk about her career.

"It's swell being a nudist," she said, "but I wouldn't want to make it my life's work. I think the whole world should go nudist in the summer. You save so much on clothes. But then I don't know. I was in a real nudist colony once, and there were a lot of big, fat men there, and some women that must have weighed a ton. No kidding, you sure do see some terrible shapes in a nudist colony. Out at San Diego, we go on duty in the colony at noon and work until nine. It's like going back to your childhood—all you do is lie in the sun and play games. It's kind of silly, too. Sometimes me and my sisters get to laughing when we figure that already more than two million people have paid forty cents to see us girls running around naked. At the colony, we are a good distance from the customers, and they stand up there at the fence and strain their eyes. Sometimes I say to Ruthie, 'Ruthie, one of those psychologists would have a picnic down here.' "

By the time I got ready to go, my cold had vanished. Miss Cubitt went to the door with me. We were standing in the hall, shaking hands, when an elderly couple, a man and a woman, came out of a nearby room and started down the hall to the elevator. When they saw Miss Cubitt, their chins dropped. When they walked past us, they turned and stared. They did not appear to disapprove. They just seemed to be startled. Miss Cubitt giggled. She backed into her room.

"I guess I better say goodbye now," she said. "See you at the World's Fair."

I hope I do see her at the World's Fair, and I hope her Tiger Lily dance is successful and that she gets the reputation she wants, and I hope she makes the chin of Mr. Grover A. Whalen, president of the New York World's Fair Corporation, drop.

4. It Is Almost Sacred

Rosita Royce, 20, is a shy Methodist girl from Kansas City, Missouri, who believes so utterly in the purity of the dance she performs in night clubs behind an amazingly transparent balloon that she does not even wear the gauze-and-tape fashionable among the strip girls in burlesque houses. I talked with her in a dressing room at the Congress Restaurant.

"It takes a lot of work to fill the balloon," she said, wrapping a silk kimono tightly around her lithe figure.

Then, grunting, the dancer bent over and picked up a long rubber tube which was attached to the mouth of a treadle bellows, operated by foot-power. She fitted the end of the tube into the nozzle of the six-foot balloon behind which, ostensibly, she hides during her dance. Then she placed her bare left foot on the treadle and began to pump air into the only property, except high-heeled slippers, that she uses during her dance.

"I guess," she said, as she pumped away, "that I am the only fan or balloon dancer who really is a nudist. I mean an official nudist. Last December I organized a nudist club, the Rocky Mountain Cult, out in Denver, and we had fifty members when an engagement took me away. I believe it is healthy for the mind and the body. I think the human body is beautiful and I am not ashamed by nakedness.

"Of course, a lot of people believe that nudism, or even the balloon dance that I do, is indecent exposure. I followed Sally Rand in the Streets of Paris at A Century of Progress Exposition in Chicago and I was using my butterfly dance. The butterfly costume is made out of black lace———"

"Why, it is so beautiful it is almost sacred," said Samuel J. Burger, her manager.

"Yes," said the young dancer, "it is beautiful. And so I was dancing my butterfly dance and it was a windy night. I was out in the open air and the winds from the lake were blowing hard and they blew off the silver fig-leaf I had on. Well, the Fair police took me in and scolded me, but the real Chicago police arrested me for indecent exposure and I would have been in a terrible fix if the judge hadn't acquitted me."

Preparing for her dance, Miss Royce said that she is forced to dance behind curtains because customers would doubtless stick pins or cigarettes into the balloon if they could reach it.

"They often burst on me," she said. "In a lot of cabarets they use these steel-wool brushes on the floor and sometimes a tiny piece of wire gets caught in a crack and when my balloon hits it there is an explosion. Also the spangles from the chorus girls' dresses get caught in the cracks and break my balloon. They cost $12.50 apiece and I have to get a new one every three days."

Miss Royce travels with her mother, Mrs. Bertha Royce, a business-like middle-aged woman. Her father runs a chain of dentist offices in Kansas City. She said her real name is Marjorie Rose Lee. Royce is her mother's maiden name. She went to Wesleyan College in Lincoln, Nebraska, and studied dramatics but did not finish the course. She started dancing professionally at seven with the Portia Mansfield Dancers and traveled all over the country. She believes she invented the balloon dance at the age of ten.

"I had it copyrighted," she said. "I had a description of my dance and a photograph sent to the Library of Congress and they copyrighted it. It is No. 157,757. Of course, the balloon dance was being performed with little balloons before I was born, but not with great big six- and ten-foot balloons. Scores of girls all over the country are imitating it with what they call bubble dances."

"A balloon is not a bubble," said Mr. Burger. "It is just a piece of rubber. Our lawyer is going to try to get an injunction restraining Sally Rand from dancing with big balloons, which is our idea, but I don't know if it'll do any good."

"I don't want to fight Sally Rand," said Miss Royce.

"You are too shy," said Mr. Burger.

"I guess I am too shy," said Miss Royce, as she threw off her kimono, got behind the balloon and walked out on the restaurant's stage.

5. SALLY RAND AND A SUCKLING PIG

Sally Rand, the lithe, hearty siren from a Missouri corn farm, who has faced prison sentences, horse-whippings, and a fate worse than death in her tumultuous career as the nation's original fan dancer, sat on a divan in her black and silver dressing room at Brooklyn's Paramount Theatre and slowly rolled the flesh-colored stockings off her celebrated legs.

She rubbed her drowsy blue eyes. Then she scratched her back, grunted with satisfaction, and remarked that the make-up she applies to various sections of her body sometimes makes her itch. She said, "Doesn't it feel good to scratch?" It was very warm in the dressing room, and so she pulled the legs of her filmy pajamas up to her pink, dimpled knees, wriggled her painted toes and said, "I like to be as naked as possible."

"Only," she said, "I'm against organized nudism. I think those nudist people are selling the public a bill of goods that they are foolish to pay for. It shouldn't cost anybody anything to go naked. There was a nudist cult out on the West Coast, and their lawyer came around and offered me a big sum to go out there and endorse it. Did I give him a tongue-lashing? I ask you."

"Are you afraid of competition from the nudists?" she was asked.

"Oh, no," she said. "It's nothing commercial. The offer shocked me. I knew that if I endorsed it a lot of fat old men would join the cult just to see me without fans. It made me sick, to think that my lovely dance should be confused with such things! Those nudists told me that your moral fiber is made stronger if you go naked, but all the nudists I saw had scratches all over their rear ends where they had been sitting down on thorns."

She pushed her hands through her blond curls. Her Japanese maid, Stella Sato, a jovial, bespectacled Oriental, pattered in and began to shake out Miss Rand's ostrich fans.

"How do you feel, Stella?" asked Miss Rand.

"O.K.," said Miss Sato.

"The reason I asked her that," said Miss Rand, "is because we just made the longest overnight theatrical jump on record. Last night at 9:30 I ran off the stage of the Paramount Theatre in Omaha, Nebraska, and jumped into a pair of woolen pajamas. Then we drove to the airport, got into a United Airline plane, and rode all night. I was in time for the first show here in Brooklyn.

"I complicated things at Omaha because one of my admirers gave me a fat little suckling pig with a red ribbon around his neck. I put it in a shoe-box and punched some holes in it so he could breathe. The airline won't let you take pets. When I got in the plane the pig squealed on me, and I had to leave it behind. You never heard such squealing. Such a pretty little pig!"

Miss Rand has a new explanation for her dance, a dance in which she strides across the stage weaving a pair of fans in front of her.

"It is just my interpretation of a white bird flying in the moonlight at dusk," said the dancer, speaking huskily as if reciting a love poem. "A white bird, flying. It flies up into the moonlight. It is dusk. It flies low. It flutters. Then it begins to climb into the moonlight. Finally, it rests."

Miss Rand, who looks as if she could take the prize as the Healthiest Girl in America, breathed ecstatically. She said that the music for her dance is called "The Birth of Passion." She left her fans at the hotel this morning, but Lawrence Sittenberg, a fan manufacturer, arrived with a new pair just in time for the show.

She picked up one of the fans, laid it on her lap and caressed it. She did not get much sleep on the airplane, and her eyes were drowsy.

"I could just stretch out and sleep forever," she

said, ruffling the fan. "I have been having such a good time. I bought my mother an orange grove near Los Angeles, and I gave her a tractor for a birthday present. Her name is Annette Kisling. My real name is Helen Beck, and I was born in Hickory County, Missouri. My mother has been married twice. We grow the best apples in the world in Hickory County.

"I understand they have a new license commissioner here in town, and I hope he keeps his pants on. The other one said I was obscene. Personally, I think my dance is as lovely as anything in the world, and I would run from anybody low enough to see anything obscene in it."

The Japanese girl came into the dressing room; she was smiling, but her eyes were sleepy and bloodshot. "Time to go on, Miss," she said. The girl from Hickory County stood up and began to pull off her pajamas.

"O.K.," she said, flexing her right leg until the muscle in it bulged.

6. The Influence of Mr. L. Sittenberg on the Fan Dance

At least 90 percent of the fan dancers in this country—there are approximately 1,000 industrious professionals—are indebted to Lawrence Sittenberg.

Tacked on the walls of his crowded loft factory on the second floor of 107 West Forty-eighth Street are effusively autographed photographs of the leaders in the now-I'm-naked-now-I'm-not line. There is, for example, a photograph of Miss Thais Giroux on which she has scribbled:—"To Larry, to one who helped put me on the road to success. Sincerely, Thais." There are many frank photographs of Sally Rand, of course. She and Mr. Sittenberg are close friends. There is also, framed, a New Year's greeting card on which the demure Miss Rand pasted a tiny pair of panties embroidered with her name. On the card she wrote:—"I'm saving my money, so I'm sending you something I don't need. Sally."

"Get it?" said Mr. Sittenberg, giggling. "She don't need her panties any more. Sally is very artistic. Only an artistic girl would think up a card like that. She only sent out three of them, to her three best friends, of which I am one."

Mr. Sittenberg is engaged in an unusually spe- cialized enterprise. He manufactures fans for fan dancers. Each year he imports approximately 650 pounds of feathers jerked from the tails of ostriches in Capetown, South Africa. A lot of these soft, slinky feathers are used in orthodox theatrical costumes, but a good percentage of them are bought by fan dancers after they have been properly cleaned, tinted, tied and attached to celluloid handles.

He made the pair of fans with which tall, pout- ing Faith Bacon technically shielded her body on the night in 1930 when Earl Carroll's "Vanities" was raided by a squad of modest cops, a raid which marked the beginning of the fan dance as an American institution. He made the pair, priced at $80, with which Miss Rand shocked the farmers at the Century of Progress Exposition in Chicago.

Mr. Sittenberg's business is listed in the telephone book as "Sittenberg, Henry & Son, ostrich feathers, 107 W. 48th, BRyant 9-3960." Mr. Sittenberg is the son. His father has been ill for many years. The firm is thirty-seven years old and young Mr. Sittenberg, who is forty, has been junior partner since he was fourteen. Mr. Sittenberg's grandfather was Louis Sittenberg, the famous New York detective who was killed during a trip to Italy to bring back a Black Hand agent. His father, a millinery salesman, established the firm when ostrich feathers were used widely by fashionable women. He had no idea he would eventually become a theatrical costumer.

For many years the Sittenbergs sold their ostrich feathers chiefly to millinery firms, also making fans with fragile mother-of-pearl handles for society women. They also did special ostrich-feather jobs, making the fans used by the bridesmaids at President Woodrow Wilson's wedding, for example. The elaborate musical comedy costumes originated by Ziegfeld helped their business.

Any producer using tricky head-dresses is almost

certain to telephone Sittenberg. At one time or another the firm has turned out costumes made of feathers from practically every bird that flies, from pigeons to peahens.

Society women quit using ostrich fans a good while back, and since that custom languished nothing helped the Sittenberg firm or the ostrich-feather industry so much as the arrests of Miss Bacon and Miss Rand. The popularity of their dance caused hundreds of producers to hire young women willing to prance about a stage with nothing to hide their pristine nakedness but a half a gross of ostrich tail feathers. Soon after Miss Rand was arrested in Chicago, Mr. Sittenberg got a bale of orders for fans. Since that time he has made up almost 1,000 pairs. He has turned out eight pairs for Miss Rand. She sends them back periodically for reconditioning. He has two pairs of Rand fans in the shop now.

Mr. Sittenberg said he would rather deal with fan dancers than millinery firms.

"They are an honest bunch of people," he said. "Of course, I send them everything C.O.D., so they can't gyp me."

The ostrich-feather czar said the fan dance is nothing new, that dancers have used fans since the infancy of musical comedies.

"The only thing is they didn't do it nude, and they

used only one fan," he said. "A real fan dance like Sally does is complicated. I have figured out that there are exactly forty-eight different positions in which the fans may be held gracefully by a naked woman. I can do them all myself. I originated many of the positions myself.

"Only an artist can use these big fans. Most fan dancers, of course, just run out on the stage waving their fans and jump around like a goat. Sally is a showman. She would make Barnum look like the barker in a medicine show. She was the first of the fan women who believed enough in herself to spend money, hire a press agent and get herself known."

Lately Mr. Sittenberg has branched out. He has invented several fan dances—"Leda and the Swan is one and the Cascade, a knockout if the right girl does it, is another"—and is managing the girls who perform them. Under contract with him are Austa Sven (her real name is Myrtle Miller), who does the Swan number; Thais Giroux, hitherto an orthodox fan dancer, and Rio Grande, whose real name is Betty Adler, a Spanish fan dancer.

"She is only a few inches over four feet," he said, "and I am working out a Spanish routine for her to do with fans. The Cascade is going to be a big sensation. A nude comes out with showers of feathers around her, and she can drape these feathers into a fountain by movements of her hands. Then she can transform it into a train of feathers, or a cape. I am getting patents for these dances, so a flock of thieves will not steal them like they did the fan dance.

"All I need is a hint to originate a dance that will pull a girl out of the fan-dancing class into a big novelty or specialty number. Of course, the right kind of fan is the important thing. When I am originating a new dance there are days and days when every person in this plant is working on one fan. You can understand why one pair of Sally's fans, the pair she used in her moving picture, set her back $300. Whenever anything drastic goes wrong with Sally's fans she wires me to get an airplane at once. A few weeks ago I flew out to Milwaukee to do a job for her."

Like a matador working out a new pass with the cape, Mr. Sittenberg is concerned in a bleakly academic manner about the positions in which dancers hold his fans. He is capable of taking sides in fights between groups of fan dancers over the theory of their art, such as the war between the Western Federation of Fan Dancers, which insisted on 35-inch fans, and the United Fan, Bubble and Specialty Dancers of America, which maintained that 25-inch fans were long enough "for all dancers except those ashamed of their bodies." For amusement he goes deep-sea fishing in the boats that tie up at Sheeps-head Bay.

Sally Rand is not his most famous customer. He once turned out a nice job for Mrs. Franklin D. Roosevelt.

"It was an old-fashioned cape of ostrich feathers," he said.

CHAPTER IV

Come to Jesus

1. THE ENEMY OF RUM, ROWDY WOMEN,
SLOT MACHINES AND BIG TALK, OR WHERE WILL
YOU SPEND ETERNITY?

I admit I did not spend much time looking for one, but during eight long, sorrowful years as a reporter in New York City, years in which I covered scores of sermons and church affairs, I did not meet a minister, priest or rabbi for whom I could sincerely have any great respect. The ones who appealed to me most, however, were Father Divine, the Reverend G. Spund, and Elder Lightfoot Solomon Michaux, a gold-toothed, deep-voiced Negro, who gave up his shad and oyster peddling business in a Virginia city in 1917 to become one of the republic's most influential hell-and-damnation evangelists. I got acquainted with the Elder in Rockland Palace, an old hall under the elevated tracks at 155th Street and Eighth Avenue in which prizefights, wrestling matches and dances are sometimes held. He was holding a terrific revival in the Palace. A raucous, happy congregation of 2,500 shouted "Amen!" and "Yeah, man!" while the Elder stomped about the stage and fought sin at the top of his voice. I sat in the first row.

"I'm going to drive the devil out of Harlem and I might just as well give you people hell to start with," said the Elder.

"I bet we catch hell now," shouted a small, uninhibited worshiper in the second row.

"You done said something, brother," replied Elder Michaux. "Everywhere I turn I see people gobbling up whiskey and beer, and the men they leave their wives, and the streets are thick with gamblers. They got slot machines in all the hangouts."

Behind the evangelist sat sixty members of the "Happy Am I" choir. The self-conscious women members in the front row were dressed in olive-green uniforms with starched caps. The Elder's wife, Mrs. Mary E. Michaux, known as "the silver-tongued soloist," was also on the stage. She helped the choir sing "The Devil's on the Run" and other Michaux spirituals.

Immediately before beginning his sermon the forthright churchman instructed his ushers to go through the crowd and sell copies of the songs at 30 cents apiece. They sold hundreds of them. All the benches in the Palace were occupied.

In the rear of the hall there is a barroom, but it was boarded up when the Negro preacher leased the Palace for a week. When he was younger, Elder Michaux was a bartender in his father's saloon, but now he looks on alcohol in all its forms as a snare and a delusion.

"I see I got work to do up here," said Elder Michaux, who delivered his sermon beneath a great electric sign in which his name was spelled out in red, white and blue letters. "I got to find out where you people expect to go for the duration of eternity. I mean, heaven or hell, what's it going to be?

"And that brings to mind a problem that has been worrying some of the women I see out before me. I mean a woman marries a man and he dies, and she marries another man and he dies, and that keeps up until she's buried as many as five husbands. Well, whose wife is that woman going to be when she gets to heaven? She's got five husbands waiting for her up there, and which one is she going to mate up with for eternity?

"That's liable to cause trouble of a widespread and deep-seated nature in heaven. It would even cause trouble here on earth. That is just one of the problems I am going to take up and examine during my revival. Hear, ye."

The Elder preached until early in the morning. He chased the devil so hard he was exhausted. When he cooled off I asked him to give me some facts about himself.

He said he was born first in Newport News, Virginia, where his father kept a saloon. In 1917 he was born again. At that time he was selling seafood to the government for the mess at Camp Lee, Virginia. One day he was driving a load of shad to the camp and he felt a call to preach. That night he got some friends together and established an undenominational church and called it the Church of God.

There are seven branches of this church now. The principal church is in Washington, which is also head-quarters for his newspaper, Happy News, and his spiritual eating-house, the Happy News Café. He has a low opinion of Major J. Divine, a Harlem evangel-ist, who calls himself God.

"I am going to preach against Father Divine," said Elder Michaux. "I know he tells the people he is God, but I think he exaggerates a little. Why, he hasn't got any theology in him, that man. All he has is a lot of put-on. I know he takes in a lot of money, but I don't want money. What I want is some cabbage."

The Elder brought sixty-nine of his followers with him in a bus. He said that none of his follow-ers drinks or smokes, and that he has taught them to avoid "rum, rowdy women, slot machines and big talk." At this moment one of his followers came into the room with a cigarette in his hand.

"I had two grips, and they got mislaid," said the follower, snapping the ashes off the end of his cigarette. "Any of you all seen my grips?"

"What are you doing with that cigarette?" asked Elder Michaux.

"Oh!" said the startled follower, gazing at his cigarette. "I was just holding it for James outside. He told me to hold it for him just a minute."

"Well, throw it down and stomp on it."

"Yes, sir."

The follower threw the cigarette on the floor and stamped it thoroughly.

"I don't care if you didn't have that cigarette in your mouth," said Elder Michaux. "I don't even want you to sully your fingers with nicotine. Your body is a temple; it's not a furnace."

"Yes, sir," said the abashed follower.

2. Don't Talk When the Red Light Is On

The Reverend G. Spund makes his living marrying people ceremoniously. He calls himself "New York City's most famous marriage performer." The business is carried on in an establishment he calls "my million-dollar nuptial palace" on the ground floor of 130 East Third Street, one of the units in First Houses, the municipal low-rental housing development off Avenue A.

"When a couple books by me I give them something nice and refined, not like in a hall or a restaurant," said the Reverend Mr. Spund. "I give them a marriage they will remember, with a gold pipe organ, with an orange room and a gold room and a silver room, with a public address system, with bouquets of lilies-of-the-valley, with changing lights like in Radio City. It is a special proposition."

The Reverend Mr. Spund opened his "million-dollar nuptial palace," for which he said he paid out $10,000, in 1936, but he has been one of the city's most accomplished Jewish marriage performers for years. He estimates he has performed 10,000 marriages. He has been seventeen years in the same block and everybody in the neighborhood knows him. In addition to marriages he superintends confirmations or bar mitzvahs, and he is a hospital circumciser, a graduate mohel of the Board of Miloh.

"They come to me from all over," he said. "From the Grand Concourse they come, from Flatbush. By me a marriage means something not to forget. When a couple gets married by the Reverend Dr. Spund it does not slip the mind. Only don't write me down Dr. Spund without the Reverend before. People see that they say, 'I should be married by a doctor, no, no, no!' I am also a cantor, and I am hired by synagogues for the holidays.

"The competition is fierce in my line. In the old days when money was plenty I went to a hall and I did the marriage and for me it was $50, maybe $75, for a big wedding maybe $100, who knows? Racketeering ended that.

"It was racketeering by the big halls. A couple, maybe the parents of the couple more likely, go up to the hall to see the hall-keeper to make arrangements. Right away, of course, they start to talk prices. The hall-keeper says, 'Why should you bargain with me? For a special proposition I tell you what I'll do with you. I'll furnish the rabbi and the music with the hall.' So it is arranged.

"The hall-keeper has his own rabbi. For the marriage he hands him three dollars, five dollars. So you see where we used to get from the parents $50 now we don't get nothing, and it is all arranged between the hall-keeper and the cut-rate rabbi. So for protection we arrange our own marriage parlors, like mine here, like many big ones on the Concourse."

In 1929 the Reverend Mr. Spund established his own marriage parlor in the apartment house in which he lives, the Ageloff Towers. When the city erected First Houses across the street with federal funds he decided to rent one of the stores. In quarters originally planned for a grocery he established what he calls, according to his mood, "my wedding temple" or "my nuptial palace" or "my marriage salon." He installed an amplifying system and through it speeches and musical selections are broadcast from his little office to the wedding room. A red light goes on when the system is in use and a sign says "Don't Talk When the Red Light Is On."

Marriages are performed in the gold room. In this room is an altar beneath a canopy and 100 gilt folding chairs. Around the walls are 300 electric bulbs and during the ceremony the lights are changed from blue to red to pink to orange, etc. There are two spotlights above the altar, and they are focused on the bride and groom when they make their entrance.

"It is beautiful like a dream," said the Reverend Mr. Spund. "Everything is modernistic. My son, Jackie, aged seven, is the page boy. My daughter, Millie, she's seventeen, plays the gold organ. Also from the public address system comes music, played from records and transmitted to the wedding room. The orange and silver rooms are for the guests during the reception before and after. I don't do any catering, but there is a sweet table. They bring cakes and schnapps themselves. The whole marriage can be done for maybe $25.

"It is arranged this way. A few weeks in advance the couple comes here and sets a date by me. It must be booked in advance, like a hall. Then they go to the Municipal Building and get a license, naturally. Then the day comes, the great day, and everything is ready here. The ten witnesses, the minyan, arrive and take their places. By Jewish law there must be ten men for witnesses. Then the guests come. Then I put on my costume, and we go through the ceremony. Afterwards maybe telegrams come or somebody wants to make a speech. So that is broadcast over the amplifier.

"Then the whole party goes to a reception room. They have a glass of schnapps and wish good luck all around. Then the whole party goes to a banquet in a hotel or a hall, or the bride and groom goes right away to the honeymooning. I keep this place holy. No banquets here, no synagogue, no meetings, no catering, only this holy thing."

The Reverend Mr. Spund—his first name is Gustav—came here in 1913 from Stanislaw, a town then in Galicia but now in Poland. He is a good-natured person who wears a tiny Vandyke on his lower lip, which he strokes negligently during a conversation. He wears big nose-pinch spectacles. A black ribbon droops from them to his waistcoat.

His father before him was a rabbi, and he hopes his eldest son, Abraham, twenty, will also become a rabbi. The Reverend Mr. Spund is a member of the Cantor's Association of the United States and Canada, and a Zionist. He likes the marriage performance business.

"It is a holy business and to perform for the public such an important service in a nice way is all I ask," he said. "Such a tremendous expense I have I don't expect no fortunes, naturally. With electric bills, with rent, with polish for the floor, with a stack of bills right on time every month, I hope to make the ends meet and not much more."

3. "PEACE FATHER FRESH VEGETABLES"

The biggest businessman in Harlem is the bald, squat mulatto evangelist who calls himself, according to his mood, Father Divine, the Reverend M. J. Divine or God.

Figures concerning Divine's enterprises are apt to be capricious, but it is safe to say that he operates at least six grocery stores, ten barber shops, ten cleaning and pressing shops and a score of pushcarts selling "Peace Father fresh vegetables." He operates at least three apartment houses and ten lodging houses and is a furnished-room magnate. He also operates restaurants in which meals are laid out for 15 cents.

Some of the eggs, chickens, vegetables and potatoes sold in his restaurants and groceries and pushcarts are raised by his followers on the farms he owns in Walkill Valley, out from Kingston, New York. In the future, perhaps by next summer, he expects to supply all his followers in New York with "strictly Father Divine poultry and vegetables in season." Already trucks make regular trips to two of his four farms.

For example, each morning a battered truck from

Harlem leaves the highway and clatters up a steep, stony lane to old Hasbrouck Manor on the outskirts of Stone Ridge, a village approximately twenty miles from Kingston. Painted in red letters on the body of the truck is this legend:—"Peace. Father Divine Is God." The truck chugs up to the farmhouse, an ample stone building of three stories, which was erected by one of the original Dutch Huguenot patentees. It is one of the oldest dwellings in the United States and an Ulster County landmark. Like most of the old Dutch colonial houses in the valley, it was once painted a creamy yellow, but now it is painted gray with red trimmings and the window screens are gilded.

The driver stops in front of the house and a Negro woman, plump Mother Divine, comes down the stairs and gives him his orders. (Father Divine calls this woman "my so-called wife," insisting that only a spiritual relationship exists between them, a condition he would like to establish in the homes of all his followers.) She tells him how many eggs and chickens he can take back.

He drives to the chicken farm, a short distance from the manor house. There a crew of angels helps him pack the eggs and crate the chickens. They load the truck with bushel bags of potatoes, with vegetables freshly dug from the gardens. Perhaps one of the angels has prepared a box of strawberries or raspberries for Father Divine. Each truck takes back a gift for Divine—a dozen roasting ears, or a spring chicken for frying, or a dozen Plymouth Rock eggs. When the truck is packed the driver climbs immediately into the cab.

"Peace," he shouts, turning the truck into the lane, jubilantly steering it toward the "Peace Father" restaurants on 115th Street, on Lenox Avenue, in the heart of Harlem. "Peace. It's wonderful."

The angels go back to work. There is plenty of work to be done in this "extension of heaven." There are 145 acres on the Stone Ridge farm, and Divine is using the manor house as an office for his other farms. He has 1,500 chickens laying eggs in a row of coops, and his angels are canning raspberries and sweet corn and sowing winter roots and greens. When Divine rolls up in his blue Rolls-Royce, for which he paid $150 cash, the angels knock off work and spend as many as four hours for lunch, a meal during which they persistently announce that Father Divine is God.

After dinner Divine likes to go out and shake himself down what he calls "a bait of mulberries" from the old mulberry tree near the chicken coops. However, when his automobile vanishes down the rocky lane the followers go back to work, hitching horses to plows and chopping weeds out of the corn with the same energy they would show if they were working out a day for one of the Dutch farmers in the neighborhood. Divine is careful not to send angels to his farms unless they are handy with hoes.

Lately he has been forced to move in secrecy in acquiring farms, but lawyers and real estate dealers in Kingston agree that to date he has purchased at least 1,000 of the best acres in the fertile valley; that he paid cash for most of it; that he is in the market for more farms; that he is also dickering for a brickyard and a furniture factory.

His four farms are all within twenty miles of Kingston. He owns 145 acres in the hills of scrub oak and sumac a mile west of New Paltz. He calls this farm "the Promised Land." It is watched over by Sarah Love, a capable Negro woman, who is assisted by Dear One and Thankful Kindness.

Near High Falls he owns 165 acres and at Krumville 518 acres are to be used in the construction of a Divine city. The Sheriff of Ulster County has no idea how many angels are living on the farms, and an accurate check is impossible, as busloads come out each Sunday from Harlem and sometimes the buses return with more persons than they brought.

Divine has announced that he intends to buy up the whole valley and turn it over to "thousands and yea, millions" of his followers, an announcement regarded with apprehension by officials in Kingston.

"I will give the lots absolutely free, and if a person desires to build he can build and own his own property," Divine told one inquirer. "I mean to give you a deed for every piece you receive. That is what I am speaking of. We don't wish to have anyone involved in litigation.

"It's wonderful."

Divine has ordered the people who tenant his Ulster County property to give out no information to strangers. A reporter tried to find out how many angels lived in the Chapel Street establishment. A Negro got up from the front porch where he was painting the floor green and came to the yard. He was asked a few questions.

"I don't bear witness," he said, shaking green paint off the brush. "It's wonderful."

"Couldn't you just tell me the number of people living here?" the reporter asked.

"All information of a spiritual or personal nature will have to come from our father, who art in heaven, and I think he's in New York City right now," said the painter. "Peace. It's wonderful."

4. Except That She Smokes, Drinks Booze and Talks Rough, Miss Mazie Is a Nun

She is known as "Miss Mazie" by the blighted men who exist in the walk-up hotels along the Bowery. Her real name is Mazie Gordon, and she is a blonde with a heart of gold. Her clothing is flamboyant, and she uses cosmetics with abandon. Until midnight she sits in the cramped ticket booth of the Venice Theatre, which she owns, at 209 Park Row, with a Pomeranian dog named Fluffy in her lap.

She feeds the dog farina in hot milk, and talks to it with gruff baby talk. On cold nights she covers the dog in her lap with a blanket. She is a good business woman, and she owns the theater, a few tenements, and a few concessions at Coney Island. A chauffeur calls for her at midnight with a Stutz. She used to work in one of the burlesque houses of Hurtig & Seamon in Harlem, but she will not talk about it. She says, "I never let my right hand know what my left hand is doing."

Mazie sits in the ticket booth with a green eye-shade pulled down low over her wise, pleasant eyes. The admission to her theater, an aged moving picture house, is one dime during the day, two dimes at night. Sometimes a bum goes in at 10 o'clock in the morning, and at midnight he is still there, sleeping in his seat, snoring as if he owned the joint. Mazie does not mind, but if one begins to yell derisively at the actors on the screen, giving them good advice, she goes in and pulls him out by the slack of his worn pants.

"What the hell!" she shouts, eyeing the bum. "Maybe them other guys in there want to sleep."

Each morning Mazie gives away a double handful of currency to the inhabitants of the Bowery. A man comes up and stands before her, expectant. He is bleary-eyed. He takes off his hat and bows to Mazie.

"I thought I'd come to see you this morning," he says. "Could you let me have a nickel, Mazie, please?"

"Why don't you go die?" says Mazie, pushing two dimes through the slot in her ticket window.

"Thank you, Mazie," says the drunken man, making a speech. "Got a heart of gold. Best friend I got. Thanks, Mazie. You my girl, Mazie. See you tomorrow."

He moves off, heading for the nearest saloon.

"I got a good show on today," says Mazie. "Don't you want to see the show?"

"No, thanks," says the bum, anxious for his morning alcohol. "I got to see a man about a job."

"So long," says Mazie, closing the slot in her window.

She rubs the ears of her dog. Perhaps she takes a piece of chamois cloth from her bag and polishes her diamond rings. Perhaps she lets the usher take the window while she goes back for a drink. Perhaps she takes down one of the lives of the saints from a shelf in her booth and reads it, making change and selling tickets automatically. Mazie is Jewish, but she wants to be a nun. She admires nuns. She knows scores of nuns and many Mother Superiors, and when "The

White Sister" was playing at her theater she telephoned them all and told them to come see it free.

"I would like to be a nun and live a life of sacrifice," she says. "I am practically a nun now. The only difference between me and a nun is that I smoke, and drink a little booze, and talk rough. Except for things like that, I am a nun."

The only thing the people of the Bowery know about Mazie is that she is very kind. At night they see her take her dog for a walk in Park Row. They remember when she used to go up to Perry's drugstore in the Pulitzer Building (they are making a sporting goods store out of it now) for a cup of coffee, and they remember that she gave a nickel to every man that asked for it. Some of them know, perhaps, that she lives in Coney Island, has four sisters and four brothers. But no one knows about the days when she worked in the burlesque houses. Was she a singer? Was she a girl in the chorus? Mazie won't tell you.

"None of your damned business!" she says.

Is she married?

"I never saw a man good enough to marry, and it's none of your damned business," says Mazie.

The shopkeepers in the neighborhood—the clerks in the flophouses, the dealers in second-hand clothes, the waiters in the joints that sell a whole meal with French-fried potatoes for 15 cents—all tell stories about Mazie's generosity.

They recite with pride the remark she made to the corpulent director of one of the Bowery missions, who objected to her language.

"What makes you so damned cut up about my cherce of words?" said Mazie. "How I talk is none of your pot-bellied business."

And on the cold nights, the nights when the Bowery is the coldest street in the city, Mazie takes the bums into the Greek's on Chatham Square and buys them stew and coffee, and sometimes Mazie sees a man with busted shoes, and she turns her ticket window over to an usher and goes with the man and sees that he is shod against the wet pavements, and there is many a day when Mazie finds she has given away her profits.

But Mazie says she worries a lot, and some nights she goes home to Coney Island and cannot sleep, and for peace she looks at her religious medals and dreams of becoming a nun and reads the not especially eventful lives of the saints.

"What worries you, Mazie?"

"What worries me is none of your damned business."

CHAPTER V

Sports Section

1. "Some Bum Might Mistook Me for a Wrestler"

One Sunday afternoon I went to see Mr. Jack Pfefer, an importer of freaks for the wrestling business. He sat with his feet on the desk in a red-walled office on the tenth floor of the Times Building and carefully combed his long black hair with a pocket comb. He has worn his hair long and flowing ever since he left Warsaw to take over the management of a company of itinerant Russian opera singers.

He wore a wilted white carnation in his lapel. Some of his obese, no-necked wrestlers call him "Carnation Jack," but he does not approve of the nickname; he insists on being known as Mr. Jack Pfefer.

The red walls of his office were littered with framed photographs of wrestlers and opera singers. A sign was tacked above the rows of photographs on one wall. It read: "Dead wrestlers." Among them were photographs of several living wrestlers. When a wrestler wrongs Mr. Pfefer his photograph is immediately tacked up on the "dead wall." It is a way Mr. Pfefer has of getting even.

While the little man combed his hair he whistled a tune from "Boris Godunov." He impresses his wrestlers by whistling tunes from operas. When he finally got his hair arranged the way he wanted it, he tucked his comb into one of the pockets of his vest.

"I got to wear my hair long, like I was a poet," he said, sighing. "I don't want to be mistook for a wrestler. Some bum might come in here and mistook me for a wrestler."

The door opened and in came a member of Mr. Pfefer's herd, a mournful, furtive-mannered wrestler with a long beard who is billed only as "King Kong, the Abyssinian Gorilla Man." Even Mr. Pfefer does not know his correct name. He is a Greek, but his greatest popularity coincided with the Ethiopian war and Mr. Pfefer changed his nationality to Abyssinian. He did not mind. King Kong always looks as if he is expecting someone to hit him over the head with a chair. He always looks as if he is ready to dodge. He is popular in New Jersey arenas because of the plaintive screech he lets out when some other wrestler begins to twist his feet. He shuffled into the room and looked through a pile of letters on the desk. Mr. Pfefer jumped to his feet.

"Take off your lousy hat, you bum," he yelled.

King Kong, the "Gorilla Man" who weighs 202 pounds, obediently took off his hat.

"Go into the other room," yelled Mr. Pfefer, who weighs 125 pounds on his best days. "There's a couple more gorillas in the other room. Go inside, like I told you."

"Yes, Mr. Pfefer," said King Kong, shuffling out of the room.

"I got to handle these freaks like I was a father," said the fearless Mr. Pfefer. "They are like my little children, the bums. One day I beat them up and yell their ears off, and next day I am with them gentle like a father."

Mr. Pfefer sighed. He sighed so deeply that his wilted carnation opened up.

"This is a nervous-wrecking business," he said. "With freaks, with politics from the Athletic Commission, with fights against me all the time by the wrestling trust. Them schemers! Them manipulators! Them bums! All the time they want to squeeze me out. I lost in three years $75,000 cash fighting with them schemers, which my books can prove. They should squeeze me out! Not when I got one breath in me they should squeeze me out."

Mr. Pfefer used to be allied with the late Jack Curley, wrestling promoter and friend of the former

Prince of Wales. They fought all the time, however, and now Mr. Pfefer is alone. He calls himself a booking agent for wrestlers. Sometimes he promotes a match himself, but usually he only supplies wrestlers to matchmakers of the Garden, of Ridgewood Grove, of the Bronx Coliseum, and of the Mecca Arena, a new club which has opened up in an old theater on Fourteenth Street. Some of his boys can really wrestle, but he would not be angered if you told him that most of them could not wrestle their way out of a bathing suit, catch as catch can.

"I'm in the show business, like Ringling Brothers," he says. "The show must go on. The main thing what the public wants is freaks, a good laugh."

Mr. Pfefer claims credit for the boom in wrestling which has lasted for the last twelve years, more or less.

"On the level, on account of it's a fact," he said, "when I came on the scene the wrestling business was dead like a cemetery. Jack Curley's office was a cemetery. With me it is an art to make things boom. I have to send right away pictures to the papers. I have to change right away the names of the wrestlers. Suppose I got a boy named Alexander Garkowienko, which I did have. All right, I name him Alexander the Great, the Russian Giant. I get from Europe freaks like nobody ever saw before. Phooey! So wrestling booms. From my first match we take in from the box office a couple grand, maybe more. Before I come eight hundred dollars was wonderful like heaven. So the wrestling trust gets the credit and the glory. Do I care? The main thing what I want to make is money."

He is proud of the freaks he has imported by the ton. Sometimes he will stare at a photograph of one of his bearded, corpulent pets and shout, giggling, "Boy, what a freak." A wrestler has to be an exceedingly grotesque person to win Mr. Pfefer's respect. The wrestling business may appear wretched to some, but he usually thinks it is wonderful. Sometimes even he has a fit of loathing. He knows, however, that there is a kind of mass sadism rampant in the country, and so long as citizens will pay to see wrestlers moan and grunt and burp and slap the mat in agony he is willing to take their dollar bills. It is not a pretty business, with its epidemics of trachoma (which is an occupational disease), and its phony champions, and its catfights among promoters, and its shabby theatricalisms. It is not like prizefighting, where the best man quite often wins. About it is the furtive air of the sideshow, the flea circus.

"Oh, hell," Mr. Pfefer said, generalizing about his business, "it is like the circus with elephants that wear shoes and eat off plates. I am so sick of freaks sometimes I have to go to the opera to quit my nerves from jumping. Right now my boys are clean-living American boys. Clean-cut. One hundred percent."

A moment later, however, he was again enthusiastic about his freaks.

"I have a new monster," he said, "a freak with class. His name is Martin Levy from Boston. He has trained three months, and we got him down to 625 pounds. That is the most meat which ever stepped into a ring. He is twenty-five years old. He could not wrestle a baby-carriage but what's the difference?

"Suppose a wrestler makes a flying tackle against him, he is so big it's the same thing like you would flying-tackle the wall. Can you throw the wall? Can you pin the wall to the mat? He is expensive to me. It costs me ten, twelve dollars by the day to feed him. He eats vegetables and eggs by the dozen. He pours olive oil into his soup. He has to travel around with a truck on account of no hotel bed would hold him. By train he can't travel. It takes a half-hour to push him through the door, and suppose the train don't stop in the station only a minute? He's going to draw, you know, tremendous. If he don't draw I'm going to took him and chalk him on the wall, the bum."

For many years Mr. Pfefer had agents in Europe, men he met when he was touring with his Russian opera singers, and they would cable him whenever they caught sight of a giant who might be persuaded to come to America and wrestle. He imported his first wrestler in 1922.

"I always love sport like I love music," he said, "and I was very proud when my first giant arrived. He was Garkowienko, which I called Alexander the Great. I imported him from the Ukraine. He weighed 425 pounds when he came, but when I shipped him home he was down to 235, a ghost. Once to amuse me he took a big steel beam like they use to make skyscrapers, and he balanced it on his shoulders and sixty people stood on it, thirty on each side. He was always homesick.

"After him I bring in Ivan Poddubny, which I called Ivan the Terrible. He is dead now. He had a big mustache. His real name was Zaikin, but I thought Poddubny sounded better, more class. He was also a Russian, a real Volga boatman.

"After him I bring in the famous wrestler without a neck, Ferenc Holuban, from Budapest. He was built like a barrel without no neck, shaved bald-headed. Nobody could take a headlock on him. Each time I brought in a freak with a different style, and my next one was Fritz Kley, a German, a contortion-ist. Like a snake you couldn't hold him. As a wrestler he was fair, not good, not bad. What I didn't like with him and with all these freaks was the minute they got paid it was rush off to the post office for a foreign money order. They didn't invest a cent in this country. Also, they ate too much.

"Oh, well, my friend, the show must go on, like with Ringling Brothers. The next one was Leo Pinetzki, a Polish boy. He had the longest arms in the world, an arm reach of eight feet. He was from Lodz. His disposition was good, for a freak. Next I brought in a wrestler which started the epidemic of whiskers. I give him the name of Sergei Kalmikoff, after a famous Cossack big general in Siberia. His real name was Orloff, no class. He was the original first man I brought with whiskers. After him we got a deluge. He wore a Russian blouse, and we called him the Siberian Gorilla, which he liked. He didn't know what it meant. He thought it was a title like General or Mister.

"After Kalmikoff all wrestlers had to have whiskers. You would see these college boys that took up wrestling. They would be clean-shaven, and they would look human. Then they took to leaving the hair on their faces. To make a few dollars they would look ugly. Their wives they hated them, and the children were scared. They looked like ugly monkeys. I started the style and I should complain.

"Kalmikoff was my last gorilla from Europe. After him I use only clean-cut American boys. Like I used college boys from football teams, flying tacklers. No grunts. They was like rubber balls in the ring. But sooner or later most of them got whiskers. When he sets his mind to it nobody can look so mean and ugly as a college boy."

Mr. Pfefer is a paradox. He actually does like music, and he turns up at quite a few concerts and operas. He thinks of himself as an artist, and he has a blown-up photograph of himself in a Russian blouse, staring into space—"Me when I was with the opera," he says. He used to play the piano.

"I give it up as I am a palooka player," he said. "I don't like no palooka jobs."

He carries an ivory-headed stick with a flourish, and he is sometimes mistaken for Morris Gest, which pleases him. He looks like Morris Gest with a hangover. He dresses like an opera star. He sits around his reasonably fantastic office in shirtsleeves, and he wears elastic bands around his sleeves. When he gets nervous he snaps the bands. He is intensely religious, he says. There is a mezuzah nailed up on his office door, and he touches it every time he goes out or comes in. He also has a mezuzah nailed up beside the door of his hotel room, he said. A mezuzah is a Jewish religious object, a metal strip with a tiny scroll inside. He kisses his fingers before he touches it. He is a member of Congregation Ezrath Israel, a synagogue popular with theatrical people, at 339 West Forty-seventh Street.

"I'm a steady there for years," he said. "I have my steady seat."

He said that some of his wrestlers are impressed by his piety. His father was Schoel Pfefer, one of Warsaw's sternest rabbis. He was born in Warsaw when it was still a part of Russia. He says that he sleeps only four hours a day, working twenty. He likes to eat in delicatessens around Broadway, and it delights him when a boxing writer describes the way he rips a herring asunder.

It angered him when Jim Londos, with whom he is on terrible terms, had a photograph taken sitting in meditation like Rodin's "Thinker." He thought Londos was presumptive. He tacked the photograph up among the dead wrestlers and wrote this legend on it:—"Jeemy, no use scheming. You will never come back like all this fellows on the same wall." He writes the same way he talks. The worst thing he can think to call an enemy is "schemer."

"Londos is so far from Rodin like I am from Governor Lehman," he said, snorting angrily. "He is not 'The Thinker' but The Schemer. I just changed a little bit the title."

With his stable of wrestlers—he has about sixty on his string now—Mr. Pfefer has traveled all over the republic. However, he will not stay away from Manhattan long. He thinks it is a perfect city for a man who lives by his wits, and he is content when he can sit in his office above Times Square among his photographs, among his respectful wrestlers, five minutes away from his favorite delicatessen. He expects to make another trip to Europe soon, a sentimental trip to Palestine, where his sister, Tauba Pfefer, teaches in a Hebrew school in Tel-Aviv. He carries a Palestinian coin around in his pocket for good luck. He will not stay long, however.

"With a derrick they couldn't get me from this city," he said, snapping the pink elastic band around his left sleeve. "No difference if they make me Governor of California and give me with salary an automobile."

2. Female Pug

The only lady prizefighter I ever saw was Countess Jeanne Vina La Mar. I saw her in a room at the St. Moritz. The room smelled like a gymnasium. She was wearing cleated shoes, gym pants, two sweaters and a sweatshirt. She had just come in from a jog around the Reservoir in Central Park and was sweating like a field hand. For the first ten minutes I was in the room the Countess sat placidly on a sofa, her hands folded demurely in the lap of her gym pants, and told how she had been persecuted by Jack Dempsey (he wouldn't help her get fights), the owners of Madison Square Garden, the New York State Boxing Commission, Hollywood and the American public.

Suddenly she leaped upon a rug and began shadow boxing. Following up a terrific left jab, the Countess knocked a painting of a pirate off her grand piano. Then, mildly startled, she sat down again. She explained how it feels to be the unchallenged champion female bantamweight and featherweight boxer of the civilized world.

"Look at me!" she cried, thumping her stomach to show that it is as substantial as it was in 1923, when she began begging female cinema stars to challenge her. "Look at me! I am quick as a panther. In all my years in the ring I have never been smacked down. I am ladylike, modest and a world's sensation. I have made boxing a beautiful sport.

"Look at those muscles! How do you think I got them? I got them fighting with plug-uglies. Always with men. I can't get a fight with a woman. I brought boxing into the realm of art, and what did I get out of it? Not a cent and no appreciation and no respect. They still consider it no good for women to box. Has it hurt me? I ask you. Are my ears cauliflowered? Don't I look like a lady?"

The Countess has a license good in New Jersey and Pennsylvania. The New York commissioners have been holding out on her. She does not need a license in Florida, and so most of her exhibitions are held there.

Her most famous fight, in fact, was held in Florida. This ring battle of the century was held in Miami in 1931 and her opponent was the late W. L. Young Stribling. Johnny Risko, who refereed, called the three-round fight a draw. The Countess agreed.

"Stribling was a tough baby," said the Countess. "He gave me a poke in the eye, the bum. In the first place, I don't like to fight with men. And when I fight them I want it called an exhibition and not a contest. They called the fight with Stribling a contest. I was in the ring before I found out, and I said, 'I beg your pardon, but this is just an exhibition.' Then I stung Stribling with a solid right to the jaw, and he woke up. He put up a stiff fight."

The Countess does not sanction prizefights between women in burlesque houses or on the vaude-ville stage. She thinks women should be allowed to fight at Madison Square Garden, but her enemy, Jimmy Johnson, is strictly against the idea. And it has been difficult for her to find an opponent. She has challenged Mary Pickford, Clara Bow and most of the huskier female stars without success. They do not answer her letters.

"I would like to have one round with Clara Bow," said the Countess.

She said that her other interest is the Vina Science Health and Art League, of which she is the president, founder and organizer. She works out in her apartment and in Central Park. She jogs and prances around the Reservoir every morning.

She is a French-American. She married an Italian count when she was fourteen and came to the United States the next year. She said she has always left the underworld alone and has always fought clean. She feels she has been persecuted.

She is a dramatic soprano. When she gets tired of smacking the punching bags she sings a few songs from "Carmen." She has been married twice—once to the Italian Count and once to Paul La Mar, or "Chicago Kid" Gleason. She owns a sewing machine and makes her own clothes.

"I am just a ball of fire," said the Countess.

3. Old Ballplayer in Winter Underwear

One of the most interesting athletes I ever interviewed was the Rev. William Ashley (Billy) Sunday, the second-rate ballplayer who became the most raucous evangelist in the history of Christianity. I saw him a few months before he died, painfully, of a heart attack in Chicago. He had expanded his heart by tossing chairs around and pushing pulpits out of his way during revivals; his zealous widow once said she saw his heart under a fluoroscope in a doctor's office and

it was "tremendously enlarged." It may be blasphe-
mous to say so, but toward the end of his career I
think he got a little tired of fighting the devil. The
afternoon I saw him he lay in bed in his room at the
Salisbury Hotel and gathered strength for the old-
fashioned revival sermon he planned to deliver that
night in Calvary Baptist Church.

When I went into his room the slangy, tired old
man reached under the blankets and scratched his
back lustily.

"I got on my winter underwear," he explained. "I
can't get along without it—no, sir! I don't know
what I would do up here in New York City, N.Y., if I
hadn't put my woolen underwear in my grip."

"I just had to put Dad to bed," said Mrs. Sunday,
who insists on being known as "Ma."

"I wanted to take me a walk around town," said
the evangelist, a trifle plaintively, "but Ma made me
get in bed and take a nap. I haven't had a chance to
get around town yet.

"I had quite a few visitors. There was a sculp-
tor, and there was one of the men who ushered for
me when I held my previous meeting here in 1917,
when 65,492 souls accepted Christ as their Saviour.
That was a great meeting. We took up $120,000 in
collections."

"And don't forget," said Mrs. Sunday, "to tell
about the $100,000,000 we collected in the Liberty

Loan drive around the same time. Of course, we're not bragging, but we do feel proud of collecting that money for Uncle Sam."

"That's right," said Mr. Sunday, "and another visitor was Mickey Welch, who used to pitch for the old New York Giants years and years ago. As a matter of plain fact, he quit playing ball in 1892. I played against him many a time.

"He brought up the story about the time I was scheduled to run a race with Arlie Latham—fastest man on the St. Louis team. I was the fastest man on the Chicago team, of course. Well, in the meantime I got converted at the Pacific Garden Mission, in Chicago.

"So I was very put out, as a practicing Christian, when I heard they were going to hold this race on a Sunday afternoon. I went around to my manager and I said, 'I've been converted and I can't run in this race on a Sunday.'

"And he said, 'The hell you can't. I got all my money on that race, and if you don't win it I'll have to eat snowballs for breakfast all winter.' So I said, 'The Lord wouldn't like for me to run on a Sunday.' Well, the manager looked at me and said, 'You go ahead and run that race and fix it up with the Lord later.' "

The evangelist roared with laughter. He laughed so hard he shook the bed. Mrs. Sunday also laughed.

"So," said Mr. Sunday, "I ran the race and won."

The evangelist was asked if he drank beer when he was a baseball player.

"No," interrupted Mrs. Sunday, "he never drank any beer. The other ballplayers did, but Dad never liked it."

"Well," said the evangelist, "I guess I drank a little, but not very much. I used to like to chew tobacco, though. If a man drinks beer it creates a taste for the hard stuff and he's a drunkard before he knows it. I never would compromise with the liquor traffic.

"I believe prohibition is the best law a nation ever enacted, and it will come back, as sure as you're born. But, I don't know. I never dreamed they would destroy that law."

"Now, now," said Mrs. Sunday, "that's all done and over with. Let's forget about that."

The evangelist began to talk again about his days as a baseball player, and how efficient he was at stealing bases, and he was asked if it is true, as Heywood Broun reported, that he used to put his off heel in the water bucket when he was up to bat.

"Well, now," said Mr. Sunday, looking at the ceiling, "well, now, to tell you the truth, I never was a champion hitter. But I sure was good at stealing bases."

"And he was good at bunting, too," said Mrs.

Sunday. "I often heard how good he was at bunting. Didn't someone say that you were one of the players who originated bunting, Dad?"

Mr. Sunday did not answer. He appeared to be meditating.

"No," he repeated, "I never was a champion hitter, but I sure was good at stealing bases."

"Well," said Mrs. Sunday, "we're not talking much about religion."

"That's right," said the evangelist. "Well, seeing Mickey Welch got me to thinking about baseball. Well, young man, I'm still preaching the gospel. I been at it thirty-eight years now. No, it's been years since I preached in a tent and had a real sawdust trail. The tabernacle I had in New York in 1917 would seat 20,000 souls, and the church I'm in now only seats about 1,200. Times are changing. Nowadays, when I extend the invitation to come forward and accept Christ it's not anywhere near like it used to be years ago. Of course you have to take what you can get . . ."

"Dad," interrupted Mrs. Sunday, "I think you're tired out. I think you better go back to sleep now. You've talked too much today."

"That's right," said the obedient evangelist. He turned over on his side and closed his eyes.

4. "It Must Have Been Something He Et"

One blistering afternoon I was sitting in the dressing room of the Brooklyn Dodgers, which is reputed to be a baseball team, when John (Buddy) Hassett walked in. Mr. Hassett is twenty-five years old and he is a plumbers' helper, a crooner and a left-handed first baseman. He lives in the Bronx and to reach Ebbets Field he had to ride one hour and twenty minutes on the subway. However, he was cheerful.

He walked to his locker, and while he pulled off his green, blue and yellow necktie and his dark blue shirt he began to croon. He crooned a favorite of his, "That's How I Spell Ireland." All over the dressing room ball-players began to shout and moan. Several stuck fingers in their ears, and whimpered as if in extreme pain. Ragged Bronx cheers issued from the mouths of others.

"What is that awful noise?" shouted a ballplayer in the dim recesses of the room.

"It must have been something he et," yelled another.

"I am being haunted," yelled another.

"Why are you so cruel to us?" yelled another.

Mr. Hassett did not pay any attention to his pained colleagues. When he finished crooning about the manner in which he is accustomed to spell Ireland he began another song, "When Irish Eyes Are Smiling," which is also one of his favorites.

When he completed that number I edged up to him and asked him some questions about his art.

"I never took a lesson," said Mr. Hassett with pride in his voice. "I can croon and I can sing, but in the summer I generally croon."

"Don't you ever plan to develop this wonderful talent of yours?" he was asked.

"Why, yes indeed," said Mr. Hassett. "I expect to take some lessons in the fall. I figure I may as well capitalize on my voice. It may be the means of making me some money. On the road with the ball club I often sing. Like when we put up at a hotel where they have an orchestra the fellows usually frame me up, and I am asked to sing, which I do. Also I sang last year at the dinner of the Baseball Writers' Association. Also I have been on the program at many Holy Name Society affairs."

Mr. Hassett said he began his musical career when he was a little boy. His father, John J. Hassett, former member of the Examining Board of Plumbers and Democratic leader of the Eighth Assembly District in the Bronx, used to take him to his club, the Shamrock Democratic Club, and young Hassett would stand up and sing old Irish favorites.

"They would have beer and sandwiches after the

meeting and some entertainment," said Mr. Hassett, "and I would get up and sing. Lately, just to kid me, the members got up a petition asking me to get some new numbers."

"I imagine you are a lover of grand opera, Mr. Hassett?" I asked.

"Can't say I am," said the first baseman. "I never been to one in my life. It never appealed to me. I like to relax, and you cannot relax when you have to keep looking at a little book to find out what they are singing about. My favorite singer is Bing Crosby. I like his style.

"If I was washed up in baseball I could turn to plumbing or crooning. My father is a journeyman plumber, and I hold a plumbers' helper card in Local 463 of the Plumbers and Steamfitters Union. However, I do not like plumbing very much."

Mr. Hassett was born in the San Juan Hill neighborhood of Manhattan, where he played sandlot baseball. He moved to the Bronx in 1925. He played baseball and basketball for Manhattan College, from which he was graduated in 1933. He played with the Shamrocks and the Bay Parkways, semi-pro teams, and immediately after the graduation exercises at Manhattan he reported to the Wheeling, West Virginia Stogies. Then he played for the Norfolk Tars. The Dodgers bought him from Newark. Casey Stengel thinks highly of his ability as a first baseman and also likes to hear him sing "The Last Rose of Summer."

Music is the only subject about which Mr. Hassett is talkative. He will open up about his ability as a crooner; but about other matters he is an extremely suspicious conversationalist, weighing his answers like a Yankee farmer. Sometimes he sits for hours in the dugout without uttering a word.

"It's going to be a hot day," I said, moving out of the blazing sun.

"Well, it might get a bit warm," said the cautious first baseman, swinging two Louisville Sluggers to limber up his arms.

5. Joe Runs True to Form, but He Was Right on Louis

I had a bet on Joe Louis to win in the first round. I bet $1.50, and won $16 but it will not do me any good, because when Arthur Donovan counted ten I jumped up and knocked a table-lamp to the floor in my home and kicked over a cabinet in which I had a collection of Bessie Smith records, any one of which was worth $16, now that Bessie is dead and gone.

I drew the bet out of a pool made up in a saloon. It was a pool with thirty-two chances, a chance on Louis and a chance on Schmeling in each round and two decision chances. Each chance was 50 cents.

The first chance I bought was Schmeling in the

eleventh. I was disgusted because I do not admire Schmeling and never have, and even if he won I did not want to win any money on him. So I bought another. It was Schmeling in the eighth. I felt very tragic. So I bought another. That turned out to be Schmeling by a decision. Then I broke down and began to sob.

"You are a big fool," said the proprietor of the saloon. "You haven't got the sense God gave a billy-goat. Schmeling in the eleventh is the best chance in the pool."

I told him it was against my principles to have a bet of any kind on Schmeling. I have always admired Joe Louis, not only because he is a great fighter, but because he never says an unnecessary word. I am not that way. I am always putting my foot in my mouth. If I am in a roomful of people and there is something that absolutely shouldn't be said in that room, I always say it; I never miss.

So I stood there at the bar, with three chances on Schmeling, feeling very tragic and down and out. Then a copyreader who hangs out in the saloon heard I had Schmeling in the eleventh.

"You want to swap?" he asked. "I got Louis in the first."

"Don't say any more," I said.

So that is how I bet on Louis in the first round. By nightfall I will be telling people that I not only had a bet on Louis in the first round, but that I had bet on him to knock out Schmeling in two minutes and four seconds. Even now I think I am a fight expert. By next week I will be applying for Arthur Donovan's job.

However, I wish I had not broken all of my Bessie Smith records.

6. HARLEM IS PACKED FOR THE FIGHT

The bars, poolrooms, sporting cafés, and basement cabarets of Harlem were packed tight today with loud-laughing citizens from the Negro sections of every large city in the United States, but they were all too busy shaping up their bets and making flamboyant predictions about the horrible state Max Baer will be in when Joe Louis gets through with him to shoot pool or eat fried fish.

Harlem was described as "looking like a corn patch when the fence broke down and the milk-cows got in" by Gill Holton, the Lenox Avenue gambler, who has opened and lost three cabarets since repeal closed up his famous establishment, the Broken Leg and Busted Bar & Grill, which was celebrated for a brief period in 1931 as the wildest cabaret in the Western Hemisphere.

"Way I look at it," said Holton, who put three rubber bands around his wallet at noon and resolved to bet no more, "if Joe Louis loses this fight, every

Negro sporting man in this great country of ours will have teardrops in his eyes as big as oysters. Only an act of God will stop him from winning, like a tornado might come up and strike Yankee Stadium right in the belly, because you know and I know they will be a lot of mean people in that place tonight, and I don't like to be in the midst of so many mean people. Like being under some trees when the lightning is striking.

"Yes, sir, unless a tornado strikes, Joe will win. When Mr. Baer stick his head out it's going to be touched. Like a man stick his head into the dumbwaiter and a ice wagon fall on it. People up here got every cent they own put up for Joe except the money they saved to be buried with—funeral money, I mean."

Holton stood in front of the North Carolina Barber Shop, at 424 Lenox Avenue, and gave out his predictions. One of the old bartenders, James P. Melvin, seconded him.

"When I collect my money," said Melvin, who weighs 278 pounds in the summer and 302 in the winter, "I'm going down to 125th Street and get me a T-bone steak and one dozen little yellow yams and some chitterlings and crackling bread and a big pound cake, and then I'm going to work my way up town, stopping off at every eating place on the way until I get to 140th Street. When I get there I'm going to call me a taxicab and go home and see what Mrs. Melvin cooked up for me."

Every saloon in Lenox Avenue had pictures and statues of Joe Louis in the windows, except the Melon King's Inn at No. 438. In its window was a painting of a great iceberg watermelon, dripping with red juice and black seeds, and a photograph of Haile Selassie on a white horse. There was a charcoal sketch of Louis in the Southern-Oriental Café, at No. 386, and the sketch was offered as a prize to the one who thought up the best four-word title for it. Salesmen walked the streets selling little plaster casts of Louis, painted bronze, and a bent old man stood in front of the Big Apple, the most popular rendezvous of sporting figures, at 2300 Seventh Avenue, selling a life of Joe Louis.

At the Brittwood Bar and Grill, 594 Lenox Avenue, there was a big sign across the front, "Only Official Headquarters for Detroit Boosters' Club." Inside, sitting in booths, were a group of the wealthiest Negro real estate and pressing-club owners in the Middle West.

They were drinking straight rye and slapping each other on the back. One man had a wad of bills big enough to choke a dragon and at intervals shouted, "He'll go into the ring even up, but now it's 7 to 5. Bring me a drink of Old Taylor."

"Wait to tonight," said Fred D. Hudson, the manager. "Everybody up here'll be full of beefsteak and beer, and the boys will be laying bets on fights which won't happen until 1939."

Hudson's establishment is the headquarters of Jack Johnson, the former heavyweight champion, who now wears a blue beret and drinks Bourbon through a straw. Johnson was at home getting in plenty of sleep today, but he is scheduled to appear at the Brittwood at dinner time to make his prediction concerning the round in which Louis will knock Baer into the deepest part of the Harlem River.

Before the fight with Primo Carnera the former Negro champion said he thought Carnera would win, but now he is for Louis, although Louis has made it plain that Johnson's opinion does not interest him.

In the Harlem beauty parlors the romance between Louis and Miss Marva Trotter was discussed endlessly and crowds waited for her to show up at the Big Apple, but she went into hiding.

"The luckiest girl in the world is the way I figure her," said Mabel Gillmore, tapdancer and blues singer, who sat in the Big Apple and entertained the out-of-town sports with backroom tales. "I sure do feel sorry for Mr. Baer. Joe sure going to knock his eyeteeth out. Time he get through with that man he won't eat no breakfast for months and months. Dinner either."

CHAPTER VI

The Biggest City in the World

1. A Cold Night Downtown

The icy wind ripped across City Hall Park and the shawled, heavily bundled woman who sits all night beside the newsstand at the west stairway of the elevated terminal at Brooklyn Bridge reached over and threw a stick of wood into the blazing fire she keeps burning in an old oil drum.

At midnight, the wind blew color into the faces of undernourished men hurrying along Park Row for the scratch houses, the quarter-a-night hotels on the Bowery. It pushed against swinging signs above the streets and made them creak.

At 2 A.M. a homeless man walked into the Municipal Lodging House and was given the last cot in the pier-shed annex. Under the city's faded khaki blankets, 4,524 homeless men escaped the windy streets.

At 2:30 A.M. a man walked into the tiled hallway

of a Bowery hotel, tilted a pint bottle, grunted, savagely threw the bottle toward the gutter, and walked up the stairway to the second-floor hotel.

The Bowery was not deserted. Men with newspaper-covered bundles stood in hallways. In a white-tiled hamburger establishment hollow-eyed night workers sat on counter stools eating and reading newspapers at the same time.

In a coffeepot—a place which advertises, "We do not use stale coffee bags"—a crowd of taxi drivers sat drinking coffee and muttering at one another. The cold night made them irritable.

In Washington Market, under the hanging electric lights of the produce sheds, men and women examined with numb fingers the contents of refuse cans.

"It's a bad night for them," said a commission merchant, lighting his frayed cigar. "Vegetables don't go bad in cold weather. The market hawks will have a tough time filling their baskets tonight."

Except for two melancholy policemen, the wind-cleaned streets of Chinatown were deserted. In a basement restaurant in Mott Street, kept open at night for curiosity-seeking citizens, four girls and a man sat around a table reading tabloid newspapers. An Italian cook, dirty-aproned and drowsy-eyed, leaned against the swinging door leading to the kitchen and smoked a cigarette.

One of the girls applied cosmetics to her face, got

up, said, "I'll be seeing you," and left. The other persons around the table did not look up from their newspapers.

The city's night workers fought the cold wind and went about their business. Taxicab drivers waited outside of saloons, huddled behind their wheels. Scrubwomen hurried from subway stations to clean office buildings. There were lights all night in poolroom windows along Park Row.

Bartenders in market ginmills were lonesome.

"A cold night," said a West Street bartender.

"Yes."

"Funny, it was such a warm day. When I got up this afternoon I said to the old lady, I said, 'It's a warm day. It's like spring.' And she said, 'It's good pneumonia weather.' "

The bartender rubbed the bar with a towel. A customer came in, stamping his feet against the floor, blowing hard.

"The last block was the worst," he said.

"A cold night," said the bartender.

"Give me a brandy neat," said the customer.

At 3 A.M. there were only a few beds left on the women's floor of the Municipal Lodging House, a floor which overlooks the East River. In rows of narrow institution beds 165 women lay sleeping. In white cribs in one corner there were two sleeping children, a boy and a girl. Above the cribs was an exit light, a pale red bulb, and one could see that there were smiles on the faces of the sleeping children. Somewhere among the 165 women lay their mother. The little girl had red curls, and in one little hand she clutched a sticky toy, a prize from a popcorn box which lay, empty, on the linoleum floor.

Near the door a drowsy matron sat in a rocking chair. ("Somebody has to sit up all night and watch them in case one of the younger women gets to thinking about suicide.") Unable to sleep, three old women stood at a window and looked down at the murky, symbolic river. They whispered vague sentences to each other and watched the steady progress of a late tug.

Occasionally the disconnected conversation of the old women reached across the warm, quiet room. One said, "And when I was working at that lady's home in Westchester they said to clean up the cellar and I found a bottle of wine on a shelf and they fired me—not on account of I got drunk, but on account of they thought so much of the wine."

Minutes passed, and another woman said, "And I told him you people are all alike, and I said, 'If you think you can get away with that you're crazy.' " They huddled together, the three gaunt old women, and expressed themselves.

And the matron rocked back and forth in her chair, and the worn-out women snored. Poverty was an old experience to most of them. They had been intimate with poverty for years, and it did not keep them awake, but here and there a figure stirred fitfully. All night long the matron kept her vigil in the rocking chair.

On the floor below, in her office, sat Miss Ethel Hand, the head matron, an unsentimental, extremely kind lady. Night after night she watches over the city's fortune-twisted women. She makes them take showers, and she pours medicine down their unwilling throats, and she pulls them apart when they fight, and she puts the drunken ones to bed. She is Irish, and she has retained her sense of humor and her sense of decency, and a drunken woman does not horrify her.

At intervals there was the sound of steps on the stairs and a woman opened the door. Miss Hand provided a clean nightgown, a towel (a large towel, not a "charity towel") and gave them medicine if they looked as if they needed it. Now and then a drunken woman came in, austere, stumbling, talking to herself.

"In the morning she'll need iodine and aspirin," said Miss Hand.

"Most of these women are done for," she said. "Few of them will ever hold a job again. Their next stopping place will be Welfare Island or the river. They are old and the depression threw them into the street for good. Now they don't have a chance. This is their home, and their only possessions are the rags on their backs. . . ."

Another woman came in.

"I was sleeping in a hallway," she said, "and the cop came along. So I come on down here."

"Mamie sits down on the stairs of an elevated station and begs," said Miss Hand. "Then she takes it out in drinking. She doesn't like to take showers. Once a week, she says, is all right. If I didn't make them wash, the fleas would drag the blankets out of the building. They are always arguing and fighting about politics, and their husbands, and what good cooks they used to be. And we have a radio, and they argue about the different entertainers. . . ."

"Do you know them all by name?"

"They never give their right names," said Miss Hand. "The only right name they give is the name of their nearest relative or friend. They don't want to be buried in Potter's Field, you know."

Outside, in East Twenty-fifth Street, the wind blew, the cold wind from the dirty river. The wind blew dirty scraps of newspapers along the dirty street.

2. The Marijuana Smokers

I have seen a lot of shrill essays about marijuana in the newspapers lately. I found out about marijuana soon

after I came to New York City. One Saturday night in
1930 a Negro detective took me with him on his
rounds. We went to a rent social and then we went to
a room on the sixth floor of a tenement on Lenox Avenue. In this room three expensively dressed whites—
a man with a pale, depraved face, a woman and a
girl—were smoking marijuana cigarettes, but at the
time I was so naive I did not know what I was seeing.
I just thought they were unusual-smelling cigarettes.

Later I saw the pungent narcotic peddled at fifty
cents a cigarette in barrooms in Harlem and Greenwich Village, and once I went with a policeman to
destroy some of the weeds, just beginning to bud,
in a backyard in a Spanish neighborhood in Brooklyn.
It resembled alfalfa. Policemen have found crops of
marijuana growing rankly in Central Park, on the
grounds of Welfare Island penitentiary, and in many
backyards. Marijuana cigarettes are made from the
yellow buds of the Mexican weed cannabis. In New
York City the cigarettes are called reefers, muggles,
brifo, moota and Mary Warner. Marijuana induces
hallucinations, usually pleasant, in the brain of the
smoker, and during one stage of the period of exhila-
ration the smoker may become abnormally affection-
ate. In the final stage of the reefer jag the addict
becomes depressed, feels numb, walks with a stag-
gering gait and finally goes to sleep, sleeping pro-

foundly for hours. Criminals sometimes smoke the cigarettes to lose their sense of fear. J. Edgar Hoover believes the drug is responsible for many sex crimes, and judging from the looks of some of the ladies and gentlemen I have seen smoking it I wouldn't be surprised.

I was covering the Harlem district for The Herald Tribune—the district sprawled over expanses of the Bronx and took in parts of Canada—the night I first saw marijuana smokers. A Negro detective used to drop into our shack in the Hotel Theresa and tell about his adventures. The other reporters had grown tired of hearing about his heroic deeds, so he would bend my ears. One night he offered to take me with him on his rounds. We walked up Seventh Avenue to 134th Street and turned off. We climbed a couple of flights of dark stairs in a tenement and stood at a door. The detective knocked. Inside, above the happy cries of Negro girls and men, we could hear someone making the keys of a piano tinkle and stutter, and we could sense the eager, sensuous move of crowded dancers on a crowded floor. We could smell the corn-whiskey bucket and the plate of chitterlings, and the inevitable smell of hair-straightener came through the cracks of the door into the dark hall. We waited there, hoping no one would come up the wrinkled stairway. On the steps we had passed three drunken girls and their faces were hostile. The detective laughed when no one came to the door.

"We won't wait much longer," he said.

The detective waited a few moments longer. Then he stepped back, lifted his right foot. He hit the door right beneath the knob and it bulged. Then someone opened it.

"Hello," said the detective. "I have a friend here wants to see a rent party."

The man at the door opened it wider, so we walked in, and then we could smell the whiskey very well. A man asked the detective for a cigarette, but he did not have any.

"No tengo tobaco, no tengo papel," he said. Then he walked over to the whiskey bucket, and I ate some chitterlings. The Negroes watched us, and the piano ceased to tinkle.

Now, in Harlem, if a man cannot pay his rent, all of his friends are invited around to his apartment, whiskey and music and food are supplied, and the guests are expected to leave a little money somewhere in the room to help pay the landlord.

Rent parties are very nice affairs, but the trouble is: some people can't be satisfied, they give a rent party every night. A man's dwelling place becomes a cabaret. So the detectives have to visit around and quiet people down at 3 o'clock.

When the detective finished his cup of corn whiskey and ginger ale—he drank it from a cup because there were no more glasses around—he felt affable. All the people in the room were watching him. He motioned to the dwarf at the piano to play, and began to whistle. He walked out, began to step nimbly like a race horse. "Let's have some of yo' bad, bad music, black boy," he said to the man at the piano, who smiled and fumbled expertly with the keys. Softly, almost slyly, couples began to move about on the floor. Too tightly together to exactly dance, they moved their bodies in a melancholy undulation. Soon the mass of people in the small room were in motion. They moved slowly, then very swiftly. One man danced with two women. Besides the piano there was a man with a scar on his face, toying insanely with a trap drum. The room was dark and filled with smoke. The electric light bulbs were covered with red crepe paper. With the motion and the music the faces of the dancers changed. They crept stealthily about the floor, moving unconsciously. I was standing by the fireplace, eating a hard piece of fried chicken. In the huddle of faces, I could see my friend, the detective, dancing with a girl, who suddenly began to sing a sad, nervous song, "Safe-crackin' papa, don't you try them tricks on me." . . .

In a cubicle in the back room two drunken Negroes were quarreling. One of them walked unsteadily down the narrow hallway of the railroad apartment and stood at the door. Then he picked up a bottle, threw it at one of the red lights. It broke and glass sprinkled to the floor, the music ceased, the dancers became wild and hysterical, and someone slapped the drunken man flat on his back. The detective grabbed me, I was pulled through the door, and it was shut. Inside we could hear angry noises and then the piano's rattle began again. The detective smiled and lit a cigarette.

"How you like this party, white boy?" he asked.

"Fine," I said. We went down the shadowed stairway, stumbled over a drunk on the landing, and walked into 134th Street. I followed the detective down an alley, to Lenox Avenue, to another tenement. We walked up six flights of stairs and stood at another door.

He opened it and we walked in. In a corner there was a tall white woman, beautiful, well dressed. She was talking to a Negro with a violin under his arm. There was a strange, unearthly smell in the quiet room, like an incense. In a chair, with a long brown cigarette in his mouth, sat a very pale white man. Beside him, sitting on the floor, there was another white girl, young and piquant, but with a pale face, and also with a brown cigarette held between long, thin fingers. All the others were Negroes.

We stood in the entrance, waiting for a welcome.

Someone fired a revolver smokily. The bullet struck in the lintel. We both jumped outside and slammed the door.

"What the hell kind of a party is this?" I asked the detective.

"This is a nice party," he said, jerking the door open and walking back into the room. I saw that the two girls had gone away, but the white man was sitting in his chair with the brown cigarette in his mouth. Everyone was watching the tall detective. Suddenly he turned on his heel and grabbed a small, forlorn Negro. Then I saw that the fellow had a .45 in his hand. They caught at each other, and the detective kept a muscular grip on the small man's gun hand. They wheeled about the room, grappling, until the detective got one hand gripped about the gunman's neck. He began to choke him, steadily. They fell against the piano, and then the gun went off. It broke a key on the piano, and there was an explosion, and a tiny, futile tinkle came from the piano. All the people began to laugh. The detective choked the gunman to the floor, picked the pistol from his hand, and motioned me to open the door.

He pulled his sparring partner to his feet, and the three of us stumbled out of the room. As I closed the door I saw the very pale man light another dark cigarette. We walked down Lenox Avenue, and people from the night clubs began to question us, but we did not notice them. The detective was escorting the gunman to the precinct station.

"What kind of place was that?" I asked.

"That was a very nice place," the tall detective said, smiling.

3. VOODOO IN NEW YORK, N.Y.

Every Man to His Own Taste

Sometimes a conjure doctor, a Brother Paul or a Brother Daniel, mocks Western civilization by drinking the blood of a crudely sacrificed bat in a tenement room on Lenox Avenue, a room which contains electric lights and a radio. Sometimes a sacrificed black cat from which certain bones are to be plucked is boiled until the meat falls away on a stove which burns the gas of the Consolidated Edison Company.

Primitive and sometimes inhuman rituals which were spawned centuries ago in the minds of voodoo sorcerers and brought from the hot, damp stretches of West Africa to this country by slaves still are celebrated in deepest secrecy in apartments above the fried-fish cafés, saloons, beauty shops and pool parlors of Harlem.

A large amount of the herbs, roots and incense with which the various schools of voodoo practitioners in Harlem and other urban Negro communities celebrate their rites is bought across the counters of drugstores operated by white men, or from one of the three or four mail-order houses which also sell crystal balls to clairvoyants ($3 each) and ectoplasm boxes to spiritualist mediums ($15 each).

When Negro prisoners are searched in Harlem police stations their watch pockets often yield evil-smelling conjure bags, tiny cloth sacks similar to sachets and crammed with such objects as the bleached chinbones and wishbones of cats, or with messy compounds of roots and herbs. Matrons have stripped women prisoners and found them wearing silken bands from which dangled the greasy bones of animals.

Detectives have reported that at least one-fourth of the Negro prisoners searched in the West 135th Street station carry lodestones. Most lodes are roughly oval pieces of iron ore. They usually are of high metal content and with enough magnetic power to lift iron filings. Sometimes they are carried with iron filings sticking to them, and then they are called "lodes with hair on them."

A box of lodes may be bought for 15 cents, but sometimes they are sold in velvet-padded jewel boxes for $5 and $10. Among other things they are supposed to "restore lost powers."

Weirdly twisted roots are sold by women herbalists in their flats and by drugstores in the Negro sections of Manhattan, Brooklyn and Queens. These roots are sold under such flamboyant names as High John the Conqueror, Southern John the Conqueror, Queen Elizabeth root, Dragon's Blood root.

Thousands of Lucky Hand roots are sold. This root bears a resemblance to the human hand, a slightly palsied human hand, and is reputed to make the person who carries it lucky in picking winning numbers in bolita or "the digits," as the numbers lottery is known.

Most of the voodoo practiced in Harlem and other Negro communities of the North is corrupted. In many cults it is only vestigial.

There is a voodoo doctor in Harlem who uses a Hindu name, anoints his head with oils purchased from a store which also sells incense and candles to Catholic churches, "consecrates" the stick he uses in incantations with a prayer written by a minister of the Spiritual Psychic Science Church, and then goes into a mumble-jumble which ends with the sacrifice of a snake he bought in a pet store.

An anthropologist would scream if such a melange were called voodoo, but what else could you call it, except high-and-mighty nonsense?

This corrupted voodoo is carried out in Harlem under wraps. In the French Quarter of New Orleans, the voodoo capital of the United States, and in Algiers, the Cajun community across the Mississippi, the conjure doctors have elbow room in which to chant, and get drunk, and dance, and sacrifice doves and toads and frizzly roosters.

It is difficult, however, to practice unadulterated voodoo in a section so crowded as Harlem. One of the most important voodoo rites, the initiation of an apprentice conjure man, calls for the sacrifice of a black lamb in a square made by four consecrated candles. Scores of neighbors would be pounding on the door and wanting to know what was taking place, what kind of party are you having, anyhow, you bums, if a voodoo worshiper tried to sacrifice a black lamb in a railroad flat in Harlem.

Also, in what park can the Harlem conjure man dig for the strange roots he needs in his business? The stuff from which Confusion Dust is made does not grow on bushes in Central Park, and they will lock you up if you try to steal the snakes in the Reptile House in the Bronx. Where does the conjure man get the anointing oil he pours all over himself before he talks with the demons, and where does he get the smelly gums for his incense and the beeswax for his consecrated candles—the candles shaped like naked men and women?

The conjure man buys his supplies, including his snakes and his pretty little baby bats, from a supply house in Manhattan, a mail-order house in an office building on a street in the West Seventies. I talked for hours with the man who operates this establishment, but I had to promise not to use the name of the firm or the address before the man would open up. The name and address would not add anything to the story, anyway.

The man sells candles and incense to Catholic and Spiritualist churches, and he thinks his business will suffer if it is generally known that he also sells supplies to voodoo worshipers. The man is middle-aged and Jewish. He knows something about hypnotism and he used to be private secretary to a mystic, an English mystic who now has a big following out in Los Angeles. His office smells of strange, sweet chemicals. Beside his flat-topped desk there is a bookcase crammed with books on black magic, on religions, on herbs; books ranging from "The Sixth and Seventh Books of Moses" to "The Ancients Book of Magic" (price $5).

"I don't believe in a lot of this stuff," said the proprietor, shrugging his shoulders, "but I'm not a faker. I'm tolerant. I don't want anybody to make fun of my religion, so I don't poke fun myself. Every man to his own taste."

In the course of the man's explanation of his attitude toward his business a Negro woman came into the office and ordered some incense—one can of Compelling incense, one can of Black Art, one can of High Conquering, and one can of Concentration. The order came to $2.

Each of the cans had the word "alleged" printed just before the title—that is, Alleged High Conquering Incense. A girl wrapped up the order and the woman, smiling, went toward the elevator, toting enough incense under her arms to smell up the whole of New York County. Most of the company's business is done by mail, but a few customers insist on coming direct to the office.

"My business began with incense," said the proprietor. "I sold the orthodox incense and candles, but then some of my spiritualist customers began asking for different herbs and powders, and I branched out. I sell to voodoo priests, to spiritualist mediums, and to students of the occult. I even sell to some Hindu disciples of certain Tibetan schools. They practice right here in New York. You'll find them operating in old brownstone houses in the Sixties and Seventies, real learned men.

"Most of the things I sell to the voodoo people are the regular supplies, roots and drugs and books and powders for conjure bags. However, I sometimes sell bats for sacrifices. I order bats from a man in Texas. He says they are vampire bats. I don't sell snakes or doves as a regular line, but I can get them. I also sell dried sea horses and the horns of rams and holy wands. I sell wands for holy work. They are hand-carved, and they have a wooden hand at the top of the wand pointing upward. They cost $2.50.

"The horn of the ram is the same type as the Hebrews use in their ceremonies. Voodoo people use them to summon up spirits, demons and goblins. Invocators have informed us that a ram's horn is an aid to them in invoking some demon or goblin from the beyond. They sell for $3.25. People wear the dried Chinese sea horses. They sell for a buck apiece.

"We also sell earth imported from the Mount of Olives. Many voodooists and occultists use this genuine earth for dressing a candle or a sacrifice. That is, they will scatter the earth over whatever it is they want to dress. We also sell genuine sand from the Sahara Desert for the same purpose.

"We also put up special bargain offers of voodoo goods, a whole collection in one box. There is enough in the box, which sells for $2.25, to make a very powerful conjure bag. One box contains a lodestone, some lodestone powder, a pair of Adam and Eve roots, a High John the Conqueror and a Low John the Conqueror, a waahoo bark, a devil's shoestring, some consecration oil, an apostolic prayer for consecrating same and a piece of chamois with which the customer can make himself a bag to wear these things in after he has consecrated them."

Every person who depends on voodoo to any

degree carries a conjure bag. They are made of cloth, chamois or deerskin, and are filled with any object or collection of objects—roots, herbs, stones, powders or fetid gums—specified by the voodoo doctor. Sometimes the heart of a sacrificed animal is burned and the ashes poured into a conjure bag. They are supposed to be medicinal or protective. They are worn around the neck like asafetida bags.

Most people prefer to make their own from materials supplied at high-class prices by a voodoo doctor, but the company sells one ready-made at a dollar a throw, a "Southern style" herb pouch dressed with Van-Van oil, an oil which is reputed to be simply too, too. Crap-shooters pour a few drops of Van-Van on each hand and rub their palms together before rolling dice. It will, according to some authorities, drive away evil spirits, make hair grow, enable you to find addresses in the Bronx, help you pick the right numbers in bolita, make you walk straight when you are drunk, or help you shoot the balls into the right holes in a pin game. You never saw such oil.

The company sells a long line of powders for use in conjure bags. They include crossing and uncrossing powders. The phrase "so-called" is printed before the name of the powder on each label; one powder, for example, is sold as So-Called Uncrossing Powder. By this the company means it cannot guarantee that the powder will uncross you if you have been crossed (hexed, hoodooed or bewitched). You simply wear the so-called powder and hope for the best.

The powders are extremely smelly. The best sellers are Confusion, Supreme Master, Vision, Success, Oriental Lover's, Protection, High John the Conqueror, Commanding, Black Art, Fast Luck, Compelling, Invocation and Lodestone. High John the Conqueror is a peculiar, twisted root, and it is a fetish with innumerable powers and qualities.

It is sold as High John, Low John, Little John, Big John and Southern John the Conqueror. It is ground into powder for incense and conjure bags, and it is sold whole to those who want no frills. Sometimes it is ground up and put into Notre Dame Water, a water which makes peace in a home, or it may be thrown into Four Thieves vinegar, which is used for breaking up homes and for making people go crazy or away.

If, for example, you want someone to go away, a "hell of a long ways away," you put some of this vinegar in a bottle with the name of the person and throw the bottle into a river. However, most conjure men use John the Conqueror only for "white" work, such as obtaining peace in a home. They don't like to use it for "black" work, such as driving someone crazy. One doctor said, "I'm afraid John will turn on me if I use him for black work. It takes a long time to get straightened out if John turns on you."

Some of the conjure-bag powders contain ambergris and musk. They sell for 50 cents a bottle. Sometimes one person will wear three or four conjure bags at once, blending the smells of Black Art, Compelling and Fast Luck, for example, into one mighty symphonic odor fit to kill. The company also sells French Luck and Jockey Club perfumes.

One powder which is used extensively in Harlem is "landlady" or "rooming-house" powder. Technically, it is called Chinese Wash. Conjure men all over the country sell this stuff as a liquid and as a powder. A landlady has trouble renting her rooms, and she goes to the conjure man and asks for help. He engages in certain rites, jumping inside the double-circle and pounding the floor with a stick. Then he prescribes.

He tells her to go home and scrub out her house. When she has "all the evil conditions" scrubbed out she is supposed to sprinkle "rooming-house dust" all over the place. The base of the powder is a powerful deodorant.

"It works," said the proprietor of the voodoo supplies house, "because many rooming houses get smelly to outsiders while the landlady doesn't notice it at all, living in it all the time. The odor is so bad that people won't rent rooms. After cleaning and deodorizing the rooms rent much better, and voodoo gets the credit."

Powdered Human Brains

According to the latest information from the Department of Health, it is impossible to kill germs by tooting at the new moon with a ram's horn. However, conjure doctors are not interested in the latest information from the Department of Health. Even the poorest conjure man works on the assumption that he knows twenty times more than the finest medical man in the world.

Using a prescription he says he got from one of the demons who dwell beneath the three-pronged root of the world-mountain, a conjure doctor may wrap seven lengths of fresh snakeskins around the middle of a person suffering from stomach ulcers, telling him it is a sure cure for what ails him, and the treatment, of course, will have no effect on the sufferer, except that it will make him smell rather unusual.

A journeyman voodoo doctor feels competent to treat any disease or ailment that can possibly afflict any animal—man, mule or monster. Consequently, voodoo is a serious menace to the health of a community.

Little damage would be done, perhaps, if conjure men confined their medicine making to lovesicknesses—bringing two people together, for example, or making a man look O.K. in the eyes of the object of his affections through the use of Compelling powder or conjure bags filled with Adam and Eve roots or some such mess. Quite often conjure men give advice to the lovesick as good as the run-of-the-mill advice in lovelorn columns in the newspapers.

Such work, however, does not satisfy the conjure men. They want to prescribe for and treat people suffering with everything from tuberculosis to tertiary alcoholism. And, usually, the more disastrous the affliction the screwier the remedy. They will give rat's blood to people suffering with cancer and goofer-dust to epileptics.

The voodoo doctors and their voluntary or unconscious allies—the herb and root quacks and unscrupulous druggists—have wrecked the health of thousands. The Department of Health and the American Social Hygiene Association have found scores of voodoo doctors treating diseases.

The stuff they prescribe may not actually be dangerous in itself, although it often is, but their phony, often ghastly medicines always keep patients from receiving treatment that will cure them. A member of the medical staff of the Department of Health told a harrowing story about a medicine prescribed by one quack.

"A friend of mine, a doctor, was looking up a telephone number in a dingy drugstore in Central Harlem," said this man, "and while he was there a

customer came in and asked the clerk for some powdered human brain, about $2 worth.

"Without a moment's hesitation the clerk stepped
behind a partition in the rear of the store and quickly
returned with a small folded paper, the kind in which
cold powders are put up. The man paid for it and
walked out.

"My friend decided it would be worth $2 to find
out about the stuff. He asked the clerk if he had any
more for sale and said, 'What's it good for?' The clerk
said it was simply wonderful for nervousness and
sick headaches and syphilis and other diseases of the
brain.

"My friend bought some and went immediately to
a chemist. An analysis showed that my friend had paid
$2 for as much talcum powder as could be held on a
dime. Its monetary value was infinitesimal and its
curative power zero.

"People who buy this stuff are endangering their
lives and menacing the health of their families and
the communities in which they live. While they
spend their slim earnings on such worthless hokum
they are losing precious time."

Doctors and nurses from the Department of
Health have found Negroes using scores of fantastic
root and herb compounds for sicknesses. They have
found West Indians in East Harlem treating asthma

patients with a broth made by boiling lizards in milk, for instance. The remedies vary according to the sections from which the herbalists came. West Indians, for example, treat "dropsy" by bathing the sufferer in a brew of mullein leaves and salt, but Negroes from Alabama apply a poultice of castor oil and okra blossoms. The remedies are equally inefficient.

The Harlem Health Center has often had trouble in vaccinating children because their parents insisted the conjure bags they wore around their necks were better than any vaccine. Bag-wearing is not confined to Negroes, however. People of many races wear bags filled with lumps of asafetida, a fetid Persian sap, and Italians in New York wear garlic bags.

A Negro policeman at the West 135th Street station, an unusually intelligent policeman, maintains that an asafetida bag will protect the wearer against influenza. Doctors say that there may be some value in the asafetida bag—its aroma probably discourages people suffering with contagious diseases from coming near the wearer. They say also that the aroma probably discourages people who are not suffering with contagious diseases from coming near the wearer.

The use of conjure bags is widespread in every community in which voodoo has any influence. Not so widespread, of course, is the use of incantations—the orotund chanting of incoherent, mystic phrases to exorcise demons believed to be causing the pain. A conjure doctor has to be paid quite well for this service, since it involves the purchase and sacrifice of bats, snakes, goats, doves, chickens, etc. There are many women conjure workers in this line. Marie Bernard is typical. She was found guilty in Special Sessions of posing as a doctor, diagnosing diseases and prescribing remedies, and was sent to the workhouse for three months.

Marie operated in an apartment on East 109th Street. She did her work with sacred snakes, according to a policewoman who gathered evidence for Sol Ullman, the Assistant Attorney General, who prosecutes cases of illegal medical practice. The policewoman went to Marie's apartment and told her she was ill.

"You sure are," Marie replied, according to the policewoman. "Your body is diseased, and your head is filled up with a poison gas and your blood is bad. [The investigator was one of the healthiest policewomen in the department.] No doctor's medicine can help you, because all your sickness and crippled leg and arm is due to a curse put on you by a bad spirit in the other world. I see a woman's spirit, and you can never get well unless I cure you."

"How much will it cost?" asked the policewoman, shuddering.

"I will have to get a sacred snake for my treatment," said Marie, after figuring on a sheet of paper for some time. "A big one will set you back $7, and one a little bit smaller will come to $5.50, but I can get a real small one for $4. The bigger the snake the quicker you will throw off your trouble."

They decided on the smaller snake, and Marie figured the entire treatment would come to $7.25, which, she said, "does not include any charge for my power." The policewoman paid $3 on account, and Marie told her she would prepare some "influence water." On the next visit Marie was gloomy.

"After I worked with the snake the snake died," she told the policewoman. "That shows how bad your illness is. I'll have to get a $7 snake. This case is more serious than I had any idea."

She gave the policewoman a milk bottle full of a liquid which she said was "influence water," and told her to go home and sleep for two days. In the meantime she would work with the $7 snake. She told the policewoman to come back at the end of that time because "the spirits intend to cripple you like the hunchback of Notre Dame." She refused to make the incantations or to work with the snake in the presence of the policewoman.

"It would profit you nothing to see what goes on when I am alone with the sacred snakes," she said.

The next time the policewoman went to see

Marie she put her under arrest, sacred snakes and all.

A more common form of voodoo medicine is the "laying on of hands."

The conjure men who use this technique smear their hands with any one of a dozen types of oil mixtures—mixtures which may contain animal blood as well as herb juices—and then they go to work on the sufferer. These healers use the "laying on of hands" for luck as well as to heal. For example, if a client wants "fish-fry luck," or success in business, the conjurer will mix up six or seven drugs and pour them on, slapping the client meanwhile with his sticky hands.

The hand-healers are deeply respected, and a conjure man will go through torture to obtain laying-on ability. The faith Negroes have in hand-healers is indicated by the fact that Grant Biddle, a cemetery caretaker in Baltimore, reported last June 22 that the body of John D. Johnson, a celebrated Negro healer, had been dug up and the hands cut off.

The Italian Sailor and the Ectoplasm Box
The shabby, side-street depths to which voodoo has fallen in its transition from the Congo to Dixie to Lenox Avenue may be gauged by the fact that now all but the very best conjure men make use of ectoplasm boxes in their negotiations with demons.

These boxes are put up for lazy spiritualist mediums, and for the humorless magicians who expose them, by a small factory in Chicago, and are sold to conjure men at $15 a box by voodoo supply houses in Manhattan and New Orleans. When the box is lit, a smoky shape, roughly resembling a hooded man, floats upward. Even the little wax images resembling naked humans into which conjure men stick pins, inflicting long-distance torture, are made in candle molds in a Manhattan loft.

You do not have to study voodoo long to realize that it has gone sour. To work their furtive wonders the kings of gris-gris and the two-headed doctors now need something more powerful than rooster blood, or jungle drums, or the Essence of Bend-Over, or Southern John the Conqueror root, or Four Thieves vinegar, or goofer-dust, which is, after all, only earth stolen from the fresh grave of an infant sometime around midnight. The public schools have played hell with the powers of the conjure men. The most deadly enemy of voodoo is a movement upward in the literacy rate; witches find roosting places only on the shoulders of the ignorant.

The bones which compose the altars of the Harlem conjure men are likely to be beef bones or old soup bones, and the skulls they sometimes hold in their laps come from medical supply houses, like as not. In the whole country today there is not a single conjure worker with the power of Marie Leveau, the illegitimate quadroon who kept an aged, fat rattle-snake lying on her altar, who used to make policemen get down on their knees and bark like dogs when they came to her house in St. Anne Street, New Orleans, to arrest her. She had no respect for the law at all. Is there a conjure woman in Harlem who can make policemen from the West 135th Street station get down on their knees and bark like dogs? No!

There are conjure men in Harlem who claim to have sections of skin from Marie's old altar-snake, but they do not have any of her brain-grease. Marie never ordered any of her conjure goods from a supply house. She dug in the malaria swamps for her own roots, grubbing them up at exactly the right time of the year, when the sap and the moon were both just right.

Marie never rooted out any herbs unless there was some blood on the moon hanging up above her. And she didn't want any ectoplasm boxes in her way when she got ready to have a few words with the goblins. But Marie is gone (what day and what year nobody knows), leaving as disciples the strongest conjure men in the United States, but none as strong as she—leaving fiery legends which will someday take places on the brightest pages of American folk-lore.

However, old dead-and-gone Marie hasn't got

anything to do with ectoplasm boxes, which this article is supposed to be about, and will be, too, if High John the Conqueror will quit bothering me. Get out of here, High John!

The use of the ectoplasm box was described by the man who sells voodoo supplies but does not want his name printed because he is afraid the ministers to whom he sells orthodox incense and candles will not be as tolerant as he is. This man is very tolerant; he believes voodoo worshipers have a right to their religion and that the right is guaranteed by the Constitution. He made the same remark made by the old man who kissed the nanny goat—"Every man to his own taste." He said he sells comparatively few ectoplasm boxes because they are expensive, as voodoo goods go. For many years they were sold only to mediums, but now a good portion of the ectoplasm boxes manufactured in the United States are sold to voodoo doctors.

"I know about one demon session where an ectoplasm box was used," he said, shoving a big pile of paper-bound copies of "The Sixth and Seventh Books of Moses" out of his chair, so he could sit down.

"There was an Italian sailor who came in here and wanted some advice. He said a Harlem drugstore man gave him my address. He said he had a wife and two small daughters, and he was worried about their future. He wanted a conjure doctor to let the demons know they could have him as a sacrifice in return for ten years of prosperity. He figured he could save enough in ten years of prosperity to leave his family well fixed.

"I told him I couldn't do a thing for him, that such things weren't in my line at all. I wouldn't even give him the names of any of the doctors I know. They don't like to have strangers know their names, as a rule. However, he found a man for himself, a Negro man who used to come around to my place. This man came to me and wanted to buy an ectoplasm box, but at that time I was out of them, didn't have a one in stock. He finally got one from another doctor.

"He wanted to use the box for this client he had, this Italian sailor. I always wondered why this sailor didn't get an evil-eye woman to do the job. Anyhow, one way and another I found out everything that happened between this conjure man and the sailor.

"They went out on a Friday night. They went into some woods somewhere near Lake Hopatcong, New Jersey. The conjure man had an automobile. He took a bag with him, a bag that had a black cat in it. Well, they got into a dark place deep in the woods, up on a hill. It was a windy night, and they got to a place where the wind wouldn't hit them so hard.

"Sometime around midnight the conjure man drew

a big circle on the ground with a piece of Dragon's Blood root. It makes a red mark. Then he drew an inner circle, and between the outside and the inner circle, he wrote down the five names of God. He only knows the five names, but some know the seven names. The five he wrote down on the ground were Tet-rag-ram-maton, Yah, Seleh, Elohim and Yad-he-vey-he. That was for protection. No demon can break through a circle which has these names on it. It's absolutely impossible.

"I better tell you that I think that doctor was something of a faker. I don't believe any of the doctors can get demons to give ten years of prosperity, but you never can tell about these things. He might have been sincere. He tried hard enough, anyway.

"The doctor put three candles in the circle to form a trinity, and he prepared himself and the sailor. He anointed the sailor. Then he took and wrapped his sacred cloth around his body and tied fourteen knots in it. He wrapped the band around seven times. He put a band around his forehead. That was all for protection. You have to be careful. You never know how many demons you are going to invoke. I know a man who has invoked 130 demons personally, but that was over a period of fifteen years.

"When everything was ready the conjure man put on his invoking robes of white and stuck a cross up in the circle. Then he took the cat out of the bag and cut its throat. He and the sailor drank the blood of the cat. Then they built a fire and roasted some of the cat. The sailor got sick, but he ate enough to protect him. When that was over the conjure man began yelling and chanting and hitting the ground with this stick. After he had been chanting in this peculiar tongue for a while he turned to the sailor and told him he was in communication with the demons, and that he was trying to make the deal with them. The sailor told him to do the best he could. Then he went back to his chanting. He jumped up and down and twisted and hit the dirt with his wand. He kept talking in this tongue for a good long time. He would talk to a demon on the north edge of the circle, and then he would turn and talk to one on the south edge.

"Finally he turned to the sailor and said he had everything fixed up, that he was going to have ten years of wonderful prosperity, but at the end of that time he would have to give himself to the demons. The sailor was pleased, and he said he wanted to shake hands with the demons. The doctor told him that was out of the question, but the sailor kept insisting. He kept saying, 'I want to shake hands.'

"Well, the doctor had decided he wouldn't use his ectoplasm box unless he got into a pinch. So when the sailor kept on insisting he decided to turn on the ectoplasm. He struck a match and lit the box.

"Up into the air issued this thing, this white, filmy shape, like a man covered up with a robe. It had a shine to it. It shook a little. The doctor turned to the sailor and said, 'O.K., brother, shake hands with it.' But the sailor was writhing on the ground, gibbering. Then, all of a sudden, he jumps up and tears out of the magic circle. He was yelling in Italian and screaming like a stuck pig. The conjure man tried to catch him, but he outran the conjure man. He tore down acres of bushes getting out of the woods."

"What happened to him?"

"Well, he kept running all that night. He ran all over New Jersey and alarmed the whole countryside. Finally they caught him, and they had to put him in the insane asylum."

"What happened to the conjure doctor?"

"He kind of disappeared. I think he left town. I think he moved out West somewhere. I haven't seen him for two or three years."

4. ONE DOLLAR A BATH

In the dining room of the Home of the New York Guild for the Jewish Blind, at 332 St. John's Avenue, Yonkers, eighty-three sightless men, women and children sat down and celebrated the 109th birthday of Hirsch Smulowitz, a white-bearded tailor who called his late wife from the back room of their East Side

shop one night forty years ago and shrieked, "Re-
bekkah, I can't see!"

Mr. Smulowitz was born on February 29, 1824,
and according to the Gregorian calendar, he should
have birthdays only on leap years.

Told that he was not due a birthday party this
year, Mr. Smulowitz pounded vigorously on a table,
shouted that he would leave the home and get a job
shoveling snow. Mrs. Rose Z. Moschcowitz, director
of the home, told him there was no snow to shovel,
but his protests were so loud that she promised him
a party and forthwith ordered three big cakes.

As proud and domineering as a landed patriarch,
Mr. Smulowitz sat at the head of the table and
ordered an attendant to cut the first cake. Then he
shouted a command in Yiddish.

The attendant went at once to a cabinet, unlocked
it, brought out a bottle and poured the aged celebrant
a glass of schnapps. Mr. Smulowitz swallowed the
contents and shouted another command in Yiddish.

"On a man's birthday one glass is not enough," he
said, holding out the glass. The attendant filled it
again.

"How do you feel tonight, Reb Hirsch?" asked
Mrs. Moschcowitz.

"Not very bad," he said, tapping the table with his
glass.

"You hate to admit that you feel better than any of us," she said. Someone turned on the radio. Mrs. Moschcowitz asked him how he liked the radio.

"I don't like it," he said, emphatically. "Tell them to stop playing at once. Tell them that noise is no good."

"He doesn't care for the radio," said Mrs. Moschcowitz. "He never did. His principal pleasure is to hear someone read love stories in the Jewish newspapers. When the stories are finished, he says, 'Now read me about the market. How is the market today, maybe?'

"We have to pay him $1 to get him to take a bath. We insist that he take a bath three times a week, and it runs into money. Here lately it got to be too expensive—we have a $40,000 deficit, you know—and so we cut out a piece of parchment paper in the shape of a bill and give it to him when he refuses to take a bath. He doesn't know the difference."

"What does he want with the money?"

"His mind wanders," said Mrs. Moschcowitz, "and sometimes he forgets that he is in a home. He remembers the struggle he had to make a living in the tailor shop and he wakes up and yells, 'I haven't got money for the coal this month!'

"Every time a visitor comes to the home Reb Hirsch holds out his hand and says, 'Any money for me, maybe?' The depression doesn't interest him. He says he has been through a dozen depressions. He says it was worse after the Civil War, far worse, than it is now."

Next to schnapps and wine he cares for snuff.

He keeps a six months' supply in his pockets. The bladders of snuff cause his pockets to bulge.

Little is known about the past of Mr. Smulowitz. He was born in Riga, Russia. His wife died in 1927. For many years the Guild gave him and his wife a small pension.

After her funeral, Mr. Smulowitz was taken straight from the Brooklyn cemetery in which his wife was buried to the home in Yonkers.

He is cheerful and he likes to give orders.

On days of celebration he gets up in the middle of the floor and dances a surprisingly agile jig. He thinks he should have a glass of whiskey each day. After the celebration last night he stood up and commenced a jig. Afraid he would excite himself, Mrs. Moschcowitz asked him to sit down. He sat down, felt for his tiny schnapps glass.

"Fill it up," he said, hitting it against the table.

5. "You're Looking Better Today"

The tall, red-haired Italian-American had only one arm; shrapnel in the Argonne tore off the other at the shoulder-joint. The little Negro was sightless, blind as a rock, and there were ugly pink scars on his brown face.

The man they called Jumpy had only one leg, and it appeared to pain him to get his breath because of a little bit of gas he inhaled one morning eighteen years ago in France. He said he believes that with one pull on a cigarette you can get more smoke in your mouth than he got gas, but it still hurts. He said it hurts him a lot worse than an aching tooth hurts, or a terrible headache, and sometimes it hurts for days, hours on end.

The Italian and the one-legged man were playing checkers in the convalescent ward at United States Veterans' Hospital No. 81, at 130 West Kingsbridge Road, in the upper Bronx. The blind Negro sat on one of the iron beds with his head in his hands. He sits like that for hours on end, not moving a muscle. There were two newspapers on the bed, and both were turned to the sports pages. The two checker players stared at the board.

The war between Italy and Ethiopia had just begun, and I had been ordered to find out what veterans of the World War thought about it.

"Have you been reading about the war?" I asked the man who had swallowed gas years ago in France.

"No," he said.

"You must have read something about it."

"I don't have no interest in it," the man said. "So far as I'm concerned they can blow Europe to hell. I feel sorry for those poor Italian dopes and those dopes in Ethiopia getting their guts shot out and their heads blown off so a bunch of rich guys can make more money. Poor dopes."

"In one day they killed 1,700 men, and they wounded 3,000 over there," said the Italian-American, moving a black piece across the worn, greasy checkerboard.

"Yeah," said the gassed man.

"Where is Ethiopia?" asked the blind Negro.

"That is a lot of men to kill in one day," said the Italian-American, "but that is just the beginning. They just started."

"We killed a lot more than that in one day in our war," said the blind Negro. "There was millions killed in our war. We bloodied up the whole world."

"Would you go to war again if you were able?" I asked.

"By God," said the one-legged man, "I would not go to war for nothing or nobody. They could came over here, even Japan, and take the whole damned country and I would not go out and get my head blowed off. It wouldn't be any worse than it is now anyway."

"It is better to be in the army than starving to death without no job," said the Italian-American.

The one-legged man lit a cigarette for the Negro and handed it to him.

"A man that goes to war ain't quite bright," said the Negro. "He don't show good judgment."

I found that there was little discussion about the war in the whole hospital. The day fighting started a man said something about "those damned Wops," and an Italian veteran heard it and picked up one of the cranks they use to raise and lower the hospital beds and said he would knock the man's brains out if he didn't take "Wop" back. The man did, and there was no fight. There was more talk about the war in the wards where men are permanently confined to their beds. They were stretched out in bed with radio headphones on their heads, listening. Each bed in the hospital had a headset attached to it.

"If you want to see the guys that know about war go upstairs to Ward 2-South," said the one-legged man. "They are the guys that don't leave here until they take them out in a box. Shell shock. And look in 4-South, where they got the guys with no jaws, and their eyes and ears eaten off, and look at some of the guys with tuberculosis they got after gas burned up their lungs. Look at the T.B.'s, and ask them if they would fight again.

"Those are the guys the public never sees. They never go out of the hospital. Every once in a while one of them goes off his nut, crazy as a bedbug, thinks he's fighting again, and they transfer him to another hospital. Thousands of those guys lying in beds still fighting in France. All the public sees is a guy on crutches now and then. It don't make no difference. They can drum up another war and young fellows will trot off with smiles on their faces to get themselves blowed to hell. It's a lot of fun."

I was permitted to walk down the corridor in 2-South, but not allowed to ask questions. There was a man standing in the corridor in his bathrobe. He stared straight ahead, vacantly, and he was trembling all over. An orderly came up and guided him to his bed. A doctor said something to him. It took him long minutes to answer; the three or four words he said were uttered with great effort. The doctor said his brain is sound, but his nerves will not obey its commands. There did not seem to be much reason to ask him what he thought of the Italo-Ethiopian war.

Some of the beds in the ward had sideboards on them so the men would not fall to the floor. They have no control over themselves. Some are able to make reed baskets. They have a room at the end of the corridor in which they sit and make the baskets. Outside the leaves on the maples in the eighteen acres of hospital grounds were yellow and red, and on Kingsbridge Road kids were throwing a football about and yelling, and on the blue Hudson two young men were rowing a boat, and inside, huddled around the radiators, five middle-aged men whose nerves had been blasted out of coordination by screaming shells were struggling with reed baskets. It takes them hours to do the work a child can do in no time. It made one furious watching them struggle with the lengths of reed, trembling and fumbling.

Walking along the corridor one could see the men in their beds, staring vacantly at the ceiling. Their cheeks were sunken and pale. One man screamed and his hands reached up wildly. One man was smiling, but his eyes were as startled as if he were watching a hand grenade with the pin out.

"Hello, doctor," he said, smiling.

The doctor patted the trembling man on the shoulder.

"You're looking better today," he said.

6. Peasant Woman in Red Hook

One morning I had a good time in Red Hook, a rowdy waterfront neighborhood in Brooklyn. I went over to visit Mrs. Anna di Massa Agnese, a sturdy peasant woman from Ischia, Italy. Mrs. Agnese was eighty-one years old. She had arrived the day before on the Italian liner Rex. It was 10 o'clock when I reached the Italian-American grocery operated by her son, Salvatore Agnese, at 504 Court Street, but the old woman was still upstairs, sleeping happily in a big feather-bed. In a little while she came downstairs, rubbing her eyes. She had a wry taste in her mouth. She did not have a hangover. She said she had never had a hangover in all her eighty-one years. She went to the door of the store and spat into the street. This amused Salvatore. He sat down on a keg and laughed heartily. Then the old woman laughed.

The night before approximately sixty of her happy relatives—sons, grandchildren, great-grandchildren and assorted in-laws—gathered in the back room of the grocery and celebrated her arrival in the United States with a big dinner. During the dinner the old woman drank a large amount of home-made wine. She said the wine she drank on her way over on the Rex was too good for her taste, and so was the food. She said her son's wife, Mrs. Salvatore Agnese, was a good cook, and that the dinner—macaroni, spring chicken, rabbit, and pickled peppers—tasted better than anything she ate on the Rex.

"Tasted like home," she said, according to Salvatore, who translated every remark she made for my benefit.

"Glad you liked it, Mamma," said Mrs. Salvatore, who beamed as she rushed to get her mother-in-law a tumbler of wine.

The old lady was extremely proud of her son's grocery store. She has four sons in New York City, and they all run grocery stores. She wandered through Salvatore's store, admiring the provolone cheeses hanging in the window, slapping them affectionately with her wrinkled, capable old hands. She took the cover off the crock of black, ripe olives, and fished out a handful, eating them with relish and throwing the pits on the floor.

She was particularly pleased with the cases of spaghetti and macaroni, cases with glass fronts like sectional bookcases, cases stuffed full of many kinds of macaroni—shells, cow's eyes, elbows, seeds, butterflies, and those twisted ones known as spiedini and little crested ones known as rooster's combs (creste di gallo). She admired the cases.

"She said everything is magnificent in my store," said Salvatore, who filled his mother's tumbler with wine every time she emptied it.

"I'm glad she likes it. I've tried for years to get her to come visit us. I bet I wrote her five hundred letters begging her to come. She lives near Naples on a little plot of land, and she didn't want to leave her chickens. She has ten chickens."

The old woman broke into the conversation and talked loudly for a few moments. She was in high spirits. One of her grandchildren ran out of the back room with a drumstick in her hand. The child gnawed at the drumstick. The old woman pulled the child to her and kissed both her greasy cheeks. The child smiled with pleasure and kept on gnawing at the drumstick, enjoying it. Then the old woman began talking again.

"She says they paved the street outside her home, and now it's not so dusty any more," said Salvatore. "She says she can keep the place clean now without breaking her back. She wants to sweep out my grocery store, but I won't let her. I'm not going to let her do a lick of work. I want her to enjoy herself. I want her to eat a lot and get fat, and I want her to spend the rest of her days over here with me and my brothers."

The old woman wore a long brown dress, a sort of Mother Hubbard, with buttons down the front of it, and she had a brown shawl or bandana wrapped around her hair. Her face was criss-crossed with wrinkles, but her old eyes were clear, and she held herself erect. She went to the door of the store and looked out at the Red Hook street. She was rather bewildered by what she saw, and she came back in. She was bewildered on the trip from the pier, her son said, but when she got inside the store she felt at home. The heady smell of cheeses and olive oil made her feel right at home.

While Mrs. Agnese wandered around the store I sat on a counter and ate a piece of raw Italian ham Salvatore cut for me. When Mrs. Agnese saw me eating she came over, shook my arm, and said something or other violently. I did not know what in the hell she was talking about. Salvatore laughed.

"She said you should have a glass of wine," he said. "She said you should have some wine with the ham."

She poured me a glass of wine and smiled as I filled my big mouth with it.

Then Salvatore sat down on his keg and figured out on the back of a paper bag exactly how many children and grandchildren his mother had. After a lot of scribbling with the stub of a pencil he gave me these vital statistics:——Five sons, four of whom are in New York City; two daughters; and approximately thirty grandchildren. Once Salvatore said she had forty-three grandchildren, and once the figure was thirty-eight, but he finally settled for thirty grand-children and four great-grandchildren.

"And God knows how many cousins and things," said Salvatore, wrinkling his forehead. "She's been a widow thirty-five years. My father was a farmer. Look at her gold earrings. My father gave her those. I saw her fourteen years ago. I took my family back to Italy for her to see. She hasn't changed much. You look about the same, Mamma."

He said her sons in New York City besides him-self were Joseph, who has a grocery in Staten Island, and Gennaro and Anthony, who have groceries in

Brooklyn. The old woman will visit all her sons, going from Salvatore's house to Joseph's house. While Salvatore talked she wandered through the store, weighing things on the scales, peering into bins, opening olive crocks and stirring the olives with a big wooden spoon. She appeared to be having a good time.

7. I Know Nothing About It

All but two of the electric lights in the Dome, at 430 Sixth Avenue, a Greenwich Village meeting place for poets, painters, New York University students and other sensitive persons, were switched off and for two hours Prince Childe de Rohan d'Harcourt, a native of Guthrie, Oklahoma, stood in the middle of the floor and talked about the "cosmic ego," a force which he likened to the pituitary gland, the third eye and the submerged portion of an iceberg.

The pallid Prince appeared to be in good spirits, although he said he had been pursued by shadows and by the Police Department ever since he was separated from Miss Louise Krist, his under-age sweetheart. After their separation Miss Krist was put under the care of a woman psychiatrist at the Florence Crittenton Home. The Prince wore a purple figured shirt, a multi-colored tie and a mole-gray suit. When the Prince entered the Dome the hatcheck girl said,

"How's it, Prince?" and he bowed and said, "Quite all right, my dear."

"There seems to be a concerted effort to cause me trouble," said the poet, speakeasy decorator, ex-convict and spurious nobleman, sitting down at one of the tearoom's tiny tables and sighing. He sighed several times. Then he plunged a cigarette into a long holder and bent over to receive the fire from a match struck for him by a giggling girl.

"However," he said, sighing again, "there are about 10,000 people in this city who have learned of me since I had this trouble. They are not friends and they are not acquaintances. In fact, I have coined a new word to define them. I call them 'frantances.' I think that's a beautiful word. And, offhand, I would say 100 young women have come to express their sympathy.

"Since I was freed in West Side Court of the charge of seduction I have written many poems to Miss Krist. The best is called 'My Beautiful Bluebird.' She has blue eyes, and she dresses in blue. I am in a most deplorable situation. Miss Krist is only eighteen, but she knows she loves me. I cannot understand why her parents oppose our marriage. Oh, tears! tears! Oh, pray, how many tears are there within the ocean? I think she will get out of that home next Thursday. Then we will be married.

"Strangely a haunted singing seems to pervade the air. Tears, tears, oh, pray, how many——"

A man bent over the Prince and asked if he was ready to begin his speech.

"They are waiting anxiously," said the man, looking around at the sixty persons in the tearoom. Most of them were playing checkers, or staring at each other. The man who interrupted the Prince's discourse on tears said he was William H. Kinnaird, a former commander of the Hunts Point American Legion Post 58, and at present the Dome's master of ceremonies. He also said he was a landscape painter.

The Prince walked to the middle of the floor. He leaned on his gold-headed cane and began his speech.

"I have found," he said nasally, "the perfect original conception. Yes, in my philosophical contemplations extending over a period of twenty, or maybe twenty-five, years I have found an inner-hidden, occult thing. In most of us it is asleep. In some it has never dawned. In about once in a period of centuries it is actually wide awake, and it produces such an entity as Jesus Christ.

"Now, I must resort to words within words. Suppose we are having a little talk with a beloved, a love situation, contemplating each other in a physical way. What we are actually doing is contemplating the cosmic ego of one another. It is something like the jewel in the middle of an idol's head. You know, like the pituitary gland. It accomplishes marvelous things and no one———"

"Oh, Prince," yelled a girl in a red dress. "Should a woman tell?"

"No one," continued the Prince, disregarding the girl's query, "knows its power. It is a hidden thing. Unfortunately, it comes only one time. It is love. Now, when sensitive people do not find love the bottom drops out. It is like a boomerang. It is a matter you cannot express in the poor words we have. In fact, I assure you I know absolutely nothing about it. Look at an iceberg in the ocean. They tell me that seven-tenths of an iceberg is submerged."

"Should a woman tell?" asked the girl in the red dress.

The Prince continued. He spoke for a long time, explaining the cosmic urge from various angles. He said the cosmic urge could be looked at from any angle and it would remain the perfect, original conception. At the end of his address the master of ceremonies said the Prince would be glad to answer questions.

"Should a woman tell?" yelled the inquisitive girl.

The Prince did not look her way.

"Which would you say is the better cosmic urge?" asked a bald-headed man. "The Bulgarian or the American?"

"The cosmic urge is not confined to any one country," said the Prince. "Its qualities are ineffable."

"Should a woman tell?" reiterated the girl in the red dress.

8. Hot Afternoons Have Been in Manhattan

Coney Island Boat Leaves in Fifteen Minutes

It is a hot day. The citizens of the biggest city in the world suffer with the heat-jitters. In tenement windows tired wives rest their stout elbows on pillows and stare blankly at the raucous elevated trains. High-priced blossoms in the show-windows of Fifth Avenue florists are shriveled. Subway guards, sweating in their heavy blue coats, mutter surly curses and push people into the hot cars.

It takes ten beers to quench one's thirst. The damp, insistent heat has placed blue lines beneath the eyes of subway passengers. The flags on the skyscrapers are slack; there is no breeze.

Drowsy citizens stand in wet garments beneath the most popular thermometer in town—the giant in front of the Pulitzer Building on Park Row—and watch, fascinated, while the mercury climbs inexorably into the nineties. The asphalt in the streets is so soft that heels leave their marks in it. When two people meet one is almost certain to inquire, inanely, "Is it hot enough for you?"

Summer has the city in a stranglehold.

And the B.M.T. trains are loaded with people going to Coney Island. Almost every traveler on the Sea Beach expresses totes a little bundle containing a bathing suit and a towel. There are mothers surrounded with expectant children, and each mother has enough food for the day in a package in her lap. Before the train roars into the last station brisk young women will be smearing sun-tan oil on their faces.

And each hour one of the boats of the Rainbow Fleet leaves the big pier opposite the headquarters of the Harbor Police at the Battery.

All day a man stands at the front gate of the pier. Listen to him. "Coney Island boat leaves in fifteen minutes," he yells, holding his megaphone aloft. It is a good forty minutes before the boat will reach the Battery.

"And he kept asking me to go out with him," says a girl, laughing hysterically, "and I said, 'Oh, I know all about you.' And every time I picked up the telephone it was him again. And every time he said he loved me I said to him, 'Oh, you nasty man.' Honest, I thought I'd die."

Children whimper for ice cream and frozen custard, and their mothers slap their faces and say, "Get out of here. You can get ice cream on the boat." Presently the boat comes into sight and sidles furtively up to the pier. The gates are pulled open, and the people rush frantically aboard. They fight each other for seats on the upper deck, in the sun. In a few moments the old boat is crowded. There is not one vacant seat. Almost immediately the boat leaves its pier and begins a cool voyage of one hour. As soon as the travelers are settled salesmen begin to yell.

"Get your sun glasses," shouts a bad-complexioned youth in a white coat. "Look at my sun glasses."

"Beer and soda."

"Four times the size of a regular bar. We're selling them at 10 cents in order to advertise the new size. Get your chocolate bar."

There is a surprising number of old people on the boat. They got used to going to Coney Island when they were kids and never got over the habit. Old men in stiff straw hats sit on camp stools and read their newspapers. Stout blond women in floppy hats and black sun glasses play bridge as the boat moves through the littered water.

When the boat is tied up to the Coney Island pier, which juts far out over the breakers, the passengers rush off as if it were on fire.

Before them is one of the world's most startling sights, a spectacle as calculated to make one breathless with amazement as Niagara Falls, or a forest fire at night, or the sea itself. There are over 1,000,000 hot, happy humans on the three miles of clay-colored strand. The sand is covered with wriggling flesh. The sand is carpeted with brown, red, pink and white flesh.

Males with paunches as big as beer kegs are stretched out flat on their backs. They wriggle their toes. Enjoying the sun on their fat bodies, they grunt and yawn. Here are tall, lithe, tanned females more beautiful by far than the white, powdered girls in a night-club chorus, and here are females with figures like roll-top desks.

All of a sudden you realize that most of these humans are talking. The sound is like the sound in a theater just before the curtain goes up. Shut your eyes and listen. It is almost overpowering.

Watch a family group on the sand. They are settled around a newspaper on which is piled a mound of sandwiches, and pickles, and boiled eggs, and bananas. Watch the mother spread mustard on the sandwiches and pass them out. Watch these people as, with admirable gusto, they eat. See how they scatter sandwich rinds and greasy papers and peelings all around them.

This is the summer resort of those who have only a few nickels to spend for hot sun and sea water.

If you knew Coney Island ten years ago it is doubtful if you will find anything new there now. The freak dives on the resort's three main streets—the Boardwalk, the Bowery, and Surf Avenue—are timeless. The fat woman dies and a new one takes her place. Impregnable, the freak places withstand the half-hearted indignation of suckers and of the Chamber of Commerce.

"My friends, do not show your ignorance," proclaims the barker at the World Circus Sideshow on Surf Avenue. "If you read your daily newspapers you know that medical science stands baffled by the mystery of Serpentina, the girl without a backbone. Now, don't walk away and show your ignorance. You came down here to have a good time. Am I right, or am I wrong? I must be right. Then, my friends, see Serpentina. Born without a spinal cord. How does she live?"

Inside the crowd finds a magician, a fat woman, a tattooed man, a man with no arms. It costs extra to see Serpentina. The three members of the Sex Family sell the story of their addled lives in a plain envelope for a dime.

Down Surf Avenue there is a girl barker. She shouts for the Wonderland Sideshow. Her name is Ray Burns. She is twenty-three. She has a baby, Esther-ann, eighteen months old, and her husband, Dave Burns, drives one of the Luna buses. Wearing rehearsal bloomers and a veil, she used to stand on the platform of the Oriental, the Island's wildest girl show, and do a wriggle-dance. Now she is a remarkably efficient barker.

"They wanted me to be in a burlesque show over in New York," said Mrs. Burns, "but I'd rather be an opener down here. I feel that this job is a real opportunity."

An evangelist has opened up on Surf Avenue. He calls his place "God's Power House." At night his sign blazes out in the midst of neon lights advertising frankfurters and frozen custards. In his raucous window are posters in a variety of languages inviting the sick, blind and lame to come and get healed. And on the Boardwalk is a new sideshow billed as "Life" in large letters. Inside there is a row of human embryos in alcohol.

However, the 1,000,000 who go to Coney Island on hot afternoons are only indirectly interested in the freaks. They came for the salt water. Many of them will spend the day and night and spend no more than 25 cents. They came with their bathing suits under their clothes, or they negotiated a furtive quick change under the Boardwalk. Perhaps they brought a few sandwiches. Or maybe they will buy a few frankfurters.

Hundreds sleep all night on the strand. At any hour on weekend nights one may see young men and women dancing around fires built on the sand. One plays a mandolin. Two jump up and dance an Apache dance. Others stray away to sit beside the dubious sea water. The beach policemen testify that there are youths who spend the whole summer on the beach and never pay a nickel's rent.

A Naked Butcher on a Roof in Hester Street
The plentiful inhabitants of the lower East Side sit on the shady side of their disheveled streets and make no unessential motions.

No breezes stir. Even the gestures of the sidewalk peddlers are half-hearted. Food is cheaper on stoop stands and pushcarts in the afternoon, and now the women are going home from market—going home to their hot little kitchens. Each one carries a bulging market sack—a brown-paper sack filled with frayed vegetables.

The string of a market sack clutched in each wrinkled hand, an old wife walks slowly up Eldridge Street. Here she stops and passes a few words concerning the hot weather with another old one. Here she stops and argues for a moment with a peddler of pans.

Just above Delancey Street she pauses and gazes into the interior of a café that advertises Roumanian broilings. The establishment is alive with men. They sit around bare tables, studiously playing stuss, pinochle and Russian bank. All the hot day they have been sitting there, arguing and gambling for pennies and drinking coffee from little white cups with no handles on them. The fat proprietor sits at the cash register, drinking white wine and seltzer and grunting. The old woman walks to the doorway and peers in, frowning severely. She sees her man, a bent old person with a rusty skullcap pushed to the back of his bald head.

"So?" she says. "So you don't come home no more, is it?"

The old man grunts, tosses a card on the table.

"So you got to sit here all day?" she says, irritably. "Why? What's the reason? Don't you got a home yet?"

"Get away," the old man orders.

Muttering, the old woman moves away. Hours later the old man is still at the little table, bent over the cards. There is not much conversation in the room. An argument starts. It does not last long. The heat kills it. Most of the men are stout, but the biggest man there is Abe Haimowitz. He carries 297 pounds around with him summer and winter.

Haimowitz is proprietor of the Roumanian Grill, in the basement at 106 Forsyth Street, the lower East Side's most popular cabaret. Judges, politicians, actors and other persons of consequence go down to look at the hard-working girls in his floor show and to argue with his six waiters, all named Itzig. Haimowitz, also Mayor of Forsyth Street, looks disgusted when asked to tell how he and his neighbors spend the summer.

"At such a time you should come and ask me

that," he says, rubbing his expansive forehead with a wet handkerchief. "This is the way we spend it. Pinochle. Stuss. Pinochle. Stuss. All day long. See that guy. He played three days solid now and lost eleven cents and now he howls loud. I guess there are a whole million cafés down here, and in the summer they are full with cards. Is there anything better? You go to the shore, I ask. All right, you get burns all over. You get sand in your shoes. You get sand in your bed and do not sleep. You get stomach-ache. It is better to stay here with pinochle."

The Mayor of Forsyth Street squirts some seltzer into his white wine. The bubbles please him.

"It is hot and humidity all day down here, yes, but at night you sleep on the roof. Nothing better at all. We lay blankets down in the dark and go to sleep, everybody, all the families. The other night something terrible happened on a roof in Hester Street. There is a fat guy, so big as me almost, a butcher. He has too much to drink. He goes home and takes off his clothes. He knows his wife is up on the roof.

"He goes stumbling up there and he lifts up a blanket. It is the wrong blanket, but he does not know it. It is some other lady, not his wife. He goes right to sleep and snores very big. The lady wakes up and takes a look at him. She screams and she yells. She flees away in a hurry and almost falls off the roof. Then his right wife she gets out from under her blanket and sees him. She gives a scream. She gives him a kick, but it is no good. He snores. They call a cop, and they pull him away to his own blanket. He does not wake up. He just dreams and snores. The whole neighborhood wakes up, but not him. It is good to sleep on roof. So cool. Better yet than any shore."

The rheumatic old men shuffle their cards and mothers tote kitchen chairs into the street, and sighing, sit down, and the children play among the pushcarts. In summer the East Side lives in the street. The young mothers are in love with the sun, but the old ones sit in the shade. The babies doze in their carriages and whimper and play with their toes. The old mothers mutter unceasingly, but the young ones sit in the sun in clean print dresses and read confession magazines.

At the corner, at the foot of the elevated station stairway, there is a watermelon peddler. He has just sliced up a long, striped one, a beauty. A long slice is a nickel; a cross-slice is 3 cents. A little boy runs up to his mother and begs for a nickel. She tells him to go ask his pa. He runs into one of the stores, and his pa gives him what he wants. A moment later he imprisons his face in a slice of watermelon.

And in front of all the grimy stationery-candy stores are little pot-bellied slot machines full of sunflower seed. And the pushcart men have pans full of sliced coconut meat. The white slices float in the ice water. And children jump into the concrete troughs at which truck-horses are watered and cool themselves. And kids with shoe-shine boxes slung over their skinny shoulders make their headquarters on the stoop of the Bank of United States, at Allen and Delancey Streets. The windows are dusty, and papers are scattered about the floor inside, and the head bankers are in jail.

Down on Mulberry Street the peddlers have a round tub of ice and several bottles of flavors. They fill paper cups with shaved ice and pour the requested flavor over the steaming ice. That is gelati. And pop is more popular here than in the Jewish streets. Each store has an icebox full of pop bottles.

Angelo Rizzo sits in the cool of the afternoon beneath the electric shrine light in his undertaking parlor at 178 Mulberry Street. He smokes his cigar and plays with a tom cat.

"Not many down here go away for the summer," says Rizzo, who is Mayor of Mulberry Street. "Only to Coney. Only to Palisades Park for the day. Or maybe some families have relatives on farms up in Connecticut, and they go up to visit. And the young ones with cars go to South Beach and Midland Beach on Staten Island. The Jewish people down here they all go up to the Catskills. They got camps all through there. All over East Side is bus stations to take them to the Catskills. But the people on these streets here mostly stay home.

"The block parties and feast days they come mostly at winter. In the hot weather, myself, I eat broccoli and sheep-heads, drink barbera, do not have too much exercise, and I stand the heat with great pleasure. Barbera is the summer wine. You go into a grotto, one of them cool basement cafés, and they have a wine bottle for you. It has a compartment for ice, and one for wine. You tilt it up, and you spray your gullet. Wine is much more useful than electric fans."

Near the tenement windows bearded scholars sit in straight-backed chairs and read the Jewish holy books. They drink hot tea in glasses. The tea is so hot that a napkin is wrapped around the glass so it will not burn the fingers. It is an old East Side belief that the hotter the drink the cooler it makes you.

And in the wine stores muscatel sells for $1.50 a gallon jug, and the pushcarts stretching in a jagged line from Fifth Street to Fourteenth Street on First Avenue are piled with big onions, and bunches of dandelion, and fat snails, and bins of hardshell clams, and great wooden buckets of new pickles swimming in lukewarm brine, and dried beans in water, and twenty varieties of sun-dried fish, and grapes, and pears, and fragrant herbs.

And at night Allen Street is the promenade. At dusk it is one of the city's most beautiful avenues. In the middle is a plaza fringed with two rows of green trees and two rows of benches. Above it clatters the Second Avenue El. At night the street is crowded with young men and young women, arm in arm, or arms around each other, walking up to Fourteenth Street to see a movie, or to sit in one of the new frowsy beer gardens, or just to walk. And the kids with cars take their girls down to South Street. Mayor Rizzo says that the first few blocks of South Street are the lovers' lane of the East Side. There is a long row of parked cars there every night.

And everywhere are peddlers of kwass, the Russian beer made from bread. ("Kwass, my friends, like in Odessa," yell the peddlers.) And knishes. And ice-cream pies. And until they are too tired to see the old men sit in the cafés, drinking coffee and playing stuss. And the rabbis in shiny black coats walk by the cafés, where the old men are studiously peering at handfuls of greasy cards, and they look in wistfully. And this, vaguely, is the way the people of the East Side spend the hot days.

At the Battery Spraddle-Legged Babies
Play on the Green Grass

It is Saturday afternoon in the metropolis, and all the fortunate inhabitants have made their getaway.

The financial streets are deserted. Now and then a coatless policeman walks through Wall Street, swinging his club by its leather strap. It is so quiet one can hear, walking through a narrow street, the staccato noise of a typewriter in one of the few offices in which people still are working. No flags fly from the plentiful flagpoles. The jewelers on lower Broadway have removed their prim window displays for the weekend and pulled their shades. All the restaurants are closed. They will not open again until Monday morning.

In these narrow streets of corporations and ticker-tape there is no life.

Then one walks through Bowling Green and comes out on the Battery. The dirty, steel-blue water of the bay gleams through green trees, and the sun is on it. On the curb an aged Syrian is selling paper bags of fresh-roasted jumbo peanuts, 5 cents. The steam escapes through the little copper pipe on the peanut roaster, making a cheerful sound, and the hot peanuts smell good.

The woman at the newsstand throws grain on the pavement and the fat pigeons that roost in the eaves of the Custom House fly down, making ugly noises in their throats, and pick up the cracked corn.

And the green grass of the Battery is covered with humans. Arrogant, spraddle-legged babies run across the green grass, both arms outstretched, laughing.

Derelicts lie in the shades of the statues, sleeping off their hangovers. Now and then one of them pulls out one of the little half-pint bottles in which water-front saloons sell whiskey to the poor and takes a drink. He snorts, shakes his head and goes back to sleep. Here and there on the Battery grass one comes across one of the bottles, empty.

And the playground at the east side of the park, under the elevated tracks, is alive with children. Clerks place their babies in the swings and push them up and down, tirelessly. Kids squirm around in the skeleton-like playground contraption made of steel pipes. Little girls sit around the wooden benches and play checkers and bridge.

In one corner, aloof, a throng of older kids play the old street-game Going to Town. One kid stands still, asking questions. The others, with locked arms, dance up, answering his questions.

"What are you coming here for?" the kid sings.

"We're coming here to get married," sing the others, dancing up. "A-ransom, a-tansom, a turnable-tee."

And the park gardeners are rooting up the dead hedges. They have stacked a great, gaunt pile of hedge-bushes under the elevated tracks. And peddlers in white coats with boxes slung over their shoulders rush through the park.

"Get an Alaska pop," they yell. "Get an ice-cream sandwich. Fi' cents."

And all the benches fringing the grass are occupied. The people have had their Saturday baths and they are conscious of their cleanliness. All the colors under the sun are in the dresses of the girls on the benches.

And throngs of people from out of town are talking excitedly beneath the two bronze sea horses at the entrance of the Aquarium. Here are the people who believe that Manhattan is a good summer resort, and it is. Listen to them, and you will be bewildered by their accents.

Every hour or so one of the sightseeing buses from uptown parks near the diner at the north side of the park and a crowd gets out and walks across to stare self-consciously at the fishes. And when they come out the sidewalk photographers and the pennant peddlers and the old women with baskets of postcards and gilt souvenirs get busy.

"Get a souvenir of New York," the old women yell, proffering their baskets of gilt ashtrays decorated with the Statue of Liberty or the skyline. "Get something to take home. Only a dime."

And citizens are crowding into the Staten Island ferryboats, bound for Midland Beach, New Dorp Beach and South Beach and the other beaches on the Staten Island shore.

And all the fishing boats have pulled away from the Battery long ago. At 7 o'clock Captain Dan Bailey's

Edith left with a full load of anticipatory anglers, well equipped with sand worms and blood worms and rye whiskey. And nine times a day the white boats of the Rainbow Fleet leave Pier 1 for Coney Island, and twice a day they set off for Rockaway Beach. And when the sun goes down the hawkers for the excursion boats get busy.

"This way to the Mandalay," one shouts. "This way for the moonlight sail on the Mandalay."

Bands are playing on all the boats.

"This way to the Americana. Take a moonlight sail up the Hudson and see a Broadway showboat revue on the Americana."

On the steamer Bear Mountain there is a banner advertising the Cotton Blossom Show Boat. The decks of the excursion boats quickly become packed. And below them, on the concrete beach, ragged kids turn handsprings and beg the passengers to toss coins at them.

"Throw down a nickel," yells a kid, turning a handspring.

Someone tosses a handful of pennies. The kids fight for them. They are as fierce as fighting monkeys. If one kid gets too many the others gang and beat him. Like the boys that dive for coins off the Day Line pier at Poughkeepsie, they keep the pennies in their mouths. By the time the excursion boats leave their mouths are full.

And when the boats pull away, crowds move toward the bandstand in the middle of the Battery. It is an old-fashioned wooden bandstand in the fashion of 1900, with palings and scroll work. There are green trees with peeling trunks around the stand and the street lights throw the shadows of their green leaves on the concrete sidewalks.

And the proprietor of the refreshment stand has placed tables and the kind of twisted-wire chairs one used to see only in drugstores around his stand, and people sit there and have imitation orange drinks and listen to the music. And the sailors and their girls walk along, awkwardly kissing as they walk.

And, cursing loudly, two men begin to slug each other. They fight with abandon. A crowd gathers to give advice. Presently a policeman comes, not running, taking his time. He punches them apart with his club. They go off in opposite directions, muttering curses. The crowd dissolves.

"Song hits!" a peddler shouts. "Fi' cents."

9. No Saturday Night Sin on the Night Line

One Saturday night in the month of May I was assigned to find out if it is true what they say about the Night Line. I went up the river on the side-wheeler Trojan, of Sam Rosoff's Hudson River Navigation Corporation, the oldest steamboat line in existence.

It was the Trojan's first voyage of the season, and I spent a chaste, sober night.

The creaking old side-wheeler made a tranquil run, transporting forty-nine sedate beer-drinking passengers and a cargo of hides and wood pulp from Pier 52 in Manhattan, hard by the chicken and duck sheds of Gansevoort Market, to Steamboat Square in Albany. The Trojan has 229 staterooms and an excursion capacity of 2,000, and the forty-nine citizens who made the first trip had plenty of elbow room. Apparently it was too early in the season for Saturday night sin on the Hudson. At no time during the run were there more than seven persons sitting around the steamer's square bar, and John Quinn, the bartender, took his apron off at 11 P.M., drank a glass of Guinness for a nightcap and locked up his stock of bottles. The majority of the passengers were middle-aged and by midnight they were all in bed, and when the steamer tied up in Albany on Sunday at 6 A.M. there was not one hangover on board.

The Night Line has a wanton reputation, and I was disappointed. In burlesque the Night Line is synonymous with lechery. Remembering dozens of vaudeville and burlesque jokes about the lusty, uninhibited activities of Night Line passengers, I wandered forlornly about the windy decks for hours, witnessing nothing more pagan than a woman smoking a cigarette, the hussy. By 10 P.M. the decks were deserted. Amazed by the purity of the passengers, I retired to the saloon deck and played a pinball game with the purser at a dime a game.

The purser won eight games in a row. Then I went up to the pilot house, where bald, talkative Captain George H. Warner sat in his high chair and watched the second pilot, William Burlingham, follow the Hudson's winding channel, swinging the steamer from one side of the river to the other. As the old sideheeler—it was built in Hoboken in 1909—moved up the river, making sixteen miles an hour, he pointed out landmarks. He pointed to a tiny red light in the middle of the river and said, "That's a lantern hung to one of the stakes on a shad net. The river's full of shad this year. A fine fish; nothing better than a plate of shad for breakfast."

"I like the roe," said Mr. Burlingham. "I never yet been able to get enough shad roe."

Off Tarrytown the Captain pointed toward a distant hill. John D. Rockefeller was alive then, and the Captain said, "Old John D. lives up there somewheres. What a man! Giving away them dimes. What a man!" Off Ossining he pointed to the cheerful lights of Sing Sing Prison, chuckled and said, "That's the Country Club over there." It must have been an old joke, but both the Captain and Mr. Burlingham appeared to enjoy it. They looked up at the prison walls and laughed.

The Captain is a third-generation Hudson River man. He lives in Troy. He has been with the Night Line for forty-five years. A verbose person, he likes to recite poetry of the Edgar Guest variety to his officers, and on one wall of the pilot house he has tacked up an inspirational motto which states, "Be glad you are alive." He is outraged by the reputation given the Night Line by vaudeville comedians.

"People think the Night Line boats are full of loose women and gamblers and rum-drinkers, and it is an outrage," he said, smacking the arm of his high chair with his fist. "We try to keep that element off the boats. There is a type of woman which rides up and down the river trying to get men in trouble. We call them 'riders.' We have a watchman, and if he sees one of them riding up and down the river night after night and stirring up trouble, he politely asks her to call a halt.

"I used to go to vaudeville shows and hear them make jokes about the Night Line. All they had to do was just mention the Night Line and people would laugh. It burned me up. It is like Brooklyn. When they mention Brooklyn in a show people will laugh, but there is nothing funny about Brooklyn when you get there. It used to put me out. If I owned the Night

Line I would sue people for damages that make dirty jokes about it.

"All that talk about wild parties and gambling on our boats is exaggerated. It reminds me of a story. One night the watchman was walking past a stateroom and he heard a woman inside crying and yelling, 'Stop! Stop!' The watchman thought maybe some man had pulled a woman into his room. He knocked on the door and said, 'What's going on in there?' The man inside yelled out, 'Nothing's going on, but something's coming off! I'm pulling a plaster off my wife's back!' The watchman left in a hurry."

Captain Warner said he once took Father Divine and 2,000 of his followers up the river on the Trojan for an excursion, and it was one of the most harrowing voyages he ever made.

"It was a mess," he said, snorting. "They would get together on the decks and jump up and down and clap their hands and make them remarks about 'Peace! It's wonderful!' I went up to this Father and said, 'I think it is fine for you people to worship the Saviour, but you don't have to make so much fuss about it.' The way they were jumping up and down I was afraid they would bust the stanchions. They were a peaceful bunch except for that. They don't do any halfway job when they worship."

That night, however, life was dull on the Night Line, reminding one of the lobby of a resort hotel in the off-season. The Negro waiters, dressed in new starched coats, stood about the dining room staring gloomily at the vacant chairs. The little crowd of diners, quietly eating boiled beef with horseradish sauce or creamed chicken or mackerel, the traditional Hudson steamer dishes, displayed little gaiety as the Trojan proceeded up the river.

A few went on the deck and watched the New York Central's night expresses speeding toward Manhattan on the Hudson's east bank. A few went forward and stood beneath the pilot house, watching Captain Warner throw his searchlight on sand and gravel scows moving sleepily down the river. A few sat around the bar and drank beer and cream ale—of the forty-nine passengers only five drank whiskey.

It was obvious that they did not take the Night Line for a night of lechery. They took it for fresh air, or for a good night's sleep, or to get to Albany.

10. Execution

A bleak throng of relatives of three murderers who were to die in the electric chair huddled on the steps of Sing Sing Prison last night and waited. They passed around a quart bottle and whispered hoarsely. They still were sitting there when Robert Elliott, the State's thin, bent little executioner, trudged up the steps and entered the barred lobby.

"That's Elliott," whispered a taxicab driver, sitting

with the relatives. "That's the man that pulls the switch."

The relatives turned and stared. Elliott shook the gate and a keeper let him in. The executioner carried a little black traveling bag. He nodded to the keeper and went upstairs to prepare the utensils with which he would destroy the three men who succeeded, after a fantastic amount of trouble, in murdering Michael Malloy, the "durable barfly."

Elliott did not do as well as was expected last night because only three of the four men scheduled for death by electrocution reached the chair. Two hours before the time appointed for his death, the fourth man was given a respite of two weeks because someone believes he is a mental defective. So the State paid the executioner $450 for his night's work, instead of $600.

The three momentarily awaiting what is still referred to at Sing Sing as "the hot squat" were the principal members of the Bronx insurance-murder trust, the men who killed the barfly to get the $1,290 for which they had insured his life. That was back in February 1933. The matter was arranged in a grimy little speakeasy at 3804 Third Avenue, now a vacant store.

Anthony Marino, 28, the proprietor, needed some cash and one night he said, "Business is lousy." Frank

Pasqua, 25, a Bronx undertaker, who was standing at the bar, thought the remark over. "Why don't we insure Malloy's life and bump him off?" he asked.

Joseph Murphy, 29, whose real name is Archie R. Mott, a bartender in Marino's speak, and Daniel Kriesberg, 30, a fruit dealer, who passed a lot of time in the speak, were selected to help with the murder.

Malloy, a former stationary engineer, who had been a drunken derelict for many years, was insured. Then the murderers started treating him to poisonous whiskey. Malloy enjoyed it.

They gave him oysters pickled in wood alcohol. Malloy enjoyed them.

Then they gave him a plate of poisoned sardines into which bits of ground tin had been thrown. Malloy liked the sardines.

The barfly was stubborn. They kept feeding him wood alcohol, and one night they took him, dead drunk, to a park, stripped him to the waist, threw several buckets of water on him, and left him to die. Next morning Malloy came into the speakeasy and said, "Give me some of that good whiskey. I'm about to freeze."

Twice he was purposely run over by a taxicab. That did no good.

So, on the night of February 22, 1933, the gentle band took the barfly to a furnished room in the

Bronx, rented especially for the event, and held a gas tube in his mouth.

That killed him. Pasqua, the undertaker, got a doctor to sign a death certificate signifying that pneumonia killed the barfly. Then Malloy was buried in one of Pasqua's cheapest coffins.

But the insurance companies had the barfly's body exhumed, and so last night four men waited in the pre-execution cells. They were to be executed at 11 P.M. At 9 o'clock a telephone call came from Acting Governor M. William Bray giving Murphy two weeks' respite on the strength of his lawyer's assertion that he had new evidence that Murphy was subnormal mentally.

But no telegrams came for Pasqua, or Marino, or Kriesberg. Consequently, at a few minutes before 11 o'clock two prison vans backed up to the rear door of the prison's administration building, within the walls.

Into the vans climbed the thirty-odd men selected by the State to witness the execution of three of its citizens. The relatives, stubborn, still waited on the stone steps.

The van rolled slowly through the prison's yard and paused at the lane leading to the death house. The witnesses got out and stood under the bright lamp. They were ordered to walk single file down the lane.

At the end of the lane two guards grabbed each witness and expertly frisked him. Then the witnesses,
jostling one another to reach the front seats first,
entered the electrocution chamber.

It is a little room. On the right, as you enter, are
five benches for witnesses. The electric chair is in the
middle of the room. It rests on three sheets of rubber carpet.

There is a sign above the door through which
the doomed are escorted. It reads "Silence." At this
door stood Principal Keeper John J. Sheehy. He stood
there, red-faced, solemn, fingering the bunch of keys
at his belt. On one side of the chair was a white operating table. On the other was a wooden pail.

Frank Pasqua, the Bronx undertaker, was the first
to go. He wore carpet slippers, a gray sweater and
an unpressed pair of flannel trousers. Father John
McCaffery, the prison's Catholic chaplain, walked
beside him.

The witnesses stirred in their seats when the pale,
staring human shuffled into the room, and a keeper
said, "Silence, please." Pasqua sat down in the chair.
He did not say anything. He stared.

The priest held a cross in front of Pasqua's gray
face. Pasqua leaned slightly and kissed it.

Elliott, the executioner, came into the room. He
went to work methodically. He pulled the headpiece,

the mask, over Pasqua's face. Then he began strapping him into the chair. A keeper kneeled and adjusted the electrode to Pasqua's leg.

Elliott left the room. The switches are in another room. The witnesses could see Pasqua's fingers clutching the wooden arms of the electric chair. He clutched so fiercely that his knuckles were white.

The witnesses could hear Elliott pull the switch.

It did not last long—only three minutes.

They placed the pale little man, still staring, on the white operating table and wheeled him into the autopsy room.

Then they brought in Anthony Marino, the speakeasy proprietor who needed cash. Elliott dipped the headgear into the brine pail. He brought it out dripping. He rubbed some of the water out of it. Then he placed it on Marino's head.

Marino smiled faintly. He kissed the ivory cross proffered by the priest. He kept on smiling. He crossed his legs, but a keeper nudged him and he uncrossed them so the electrode could be fastened to his right leg.

Elliott, the precise little executioner, hurried off and threw the switch that sent 2,200 volts of electricity through Marino's body. It took three minutes.

It took only two minutes to kill Daniel Kriesberg, the wry-faced fruit dealer. He came in, not as pale as his comrades, and sat down. He was escorted by Rabbi Jacob Katz, the Jewish chaplain.

As soon as the electricity whirred into the man in the chair the rabbi left the room, holding the Old Testament firmly against his breast.

"All out," said a keeper. "Walk quietly."

The relatives still were huddled on the prison steps. They got up and stood in the shadows, aloof, as the witnesses departed. A woman among them was moaning.

One of the men drank the last whiskey in the bottle and threw it away.

The relatives were waiting to claim the bodies of the three men who helped kill a barfly for $1,290. It took them a long time to kill Malloy. It took the State only sixteen minutes to kill them.

CHAPTER VII

It's a Living

1. The Yellow Slip Shows Fifty-three Arrests

Harry Lewis, an unobtrusive, well-mannered fellow from the lower East Side, has been one of the country's most accomplished pickpockets for thirty-five years. Frequenting such crowded places as theater lobbies, rush-hour subways and skyscraper elevators at noon, he has slyly pulled wallets from thousands of pockets. He has worked in many Eastern cities and a "yellow slip" at Police Headquarters shows that he has been arrested at least fifty-three times; the slip is by no means complete.

He is forty-eight years old and he looks years younger, despite the fact that he is almost completely bald. The terse slip shows that he has worked under six aliases. The first time he was arrested he called himself Noah Berns. That was in 1901, and he was charged with being an incorrigible child. The last time he was arrested he called himself Harry Lewis.

On this occasion he was standing in a hallway of the National Broadcasting Company's studio on the eighth floor of the RCA Building in Rockefeller Center. At the time of his arrest, according to the complaint, he "had his left hand in the left trouser pocket of an unknown man." The charge was jostling.

A court stenographer telephoned me about Lewis. He said he thought Lewis was "unusually bright for a pickpocket." I went up to talk with the pickpocket in the Seventh District Jail, a grimy structure beneath the Sixth Avenue elevated tracks at 317 West Fifty-third Street. Lewis was in a cell, waiting to be sentenced. When he was taken before Magistrate Michael A. Ford in West Side Court he refused to say anything except, "I guess I'm guilty." In his cell he had two tattered wild west magazines and four packages of cigarettes. The stenographer said that when the jailer came to take him out of his cell to stand before the judge he turned down a page in one of the wild west magazines to mark his place. After putting in his guilty plea he went back to his cell and resumed his reading.

I sent in a note and Lewis consented to see me. He came out and sat for a few minutes on a dirty wooden bench facing a row of cages in which new arrivals are placed. He was an erect, muscular person, with brown eyes and regular features. He was facing three years in the penitentiary, but he did not

seem particularly disturbed by his predicament; later
I found out that confinement had ceased to bother
him. In the moving pictures a pickpocket usually is a
cringing, shifty-eyed person, but Lewis had a frank
gaze, and he spoke dispassionately about the way he
made a living. I noticed that his hands were broad and
that his fingers did not look nimble. He was dressed
in a blue suit of a Broadway cut but apparently of
good quality. His shoes and his shirt were new.

"This is the first time I ever talked with a reporter," he said. "What did you want to ask me?"

"I wish you would tell me something about your
racket," I said.

"Racket, hell!" said the pickpocket. "It's not a
racket. It's petty thievery. I never had a racket. Picking pockets is no good any more. The officers on the
P.P. Squad [the Pickpocket Squad] know my face and
I get dragged in every time they see me. It's like
butting your head against a wall."

For emphasis the pickpocket slapped the dirty jail
wall. The conversation was interrupted by a girl in
one of the cages who wanted a cigarette. The pickpocket pushed a cigarette through the cage, lit it for
the girl and gave her the package.

"I would like to have a psychiatrist go over me
because I am sure there is something wrong somewhere," he said. "I must have a twist in my brain. It

may be environment, even. I am an East Side boy and there was seven in the family and I had to get something in my belly some way. When I get a roll I am not a pickpocket any longer. I am a gambler then. When it goes the thing starts all over again."

He was asked to demonstrate the technique of picking pockets, but he refused.

"The pickpocket is regarded as the lowest type of criminal," he was told. "Do you have any pride in your work?"

"Not particularly," he said. "I would rather be a bookmaker. I like gambling better. I am more of a gambler than a pickpocket. I know I am considered the lowest type of crook, but that don't mean anything. I mean, the cops are always calling me a cockroach and squawking about how I steal a poor man's pay. Hell, I'm not the only one that steals the poor man's pay. Everybody steals the poor man's pay. There are plenty of bank presidents no better than I am."

The pickpocket's face was tanned and he looked as if he had passed several weeks on a Florida beach.

"I been in the sun," he said, "but I won't say where. I keep in shape. What gets most of the pickpockets is dope. That is the finale, when they start doping. Liquor, yes. Women, yes. But dope, no. That washes you up. When a pickpocket loses his nerve he starts doping. The most I ever done in a stretch was fifteen months, and if I could get out of this mess I would like to go straight."

"The detective said you always say you are going straight when they arrest you," I said.

"I wouldn't say that," said Lewis, with resentment in his voice. "I know picking pockets is wrong and all that sort of thing, but that's not the point. I got to eat."

I asked the pickpocket several other questions, but he grew morose and would not answer them. He volunteered some information about his life in jail.

"I sleep," he said. "I am able to sleep for weeks at a time. I think I am abnormal that way. I can sleep out a sentence."

A moment later Lewis looked at me and said, "I don't think we're getting anywhere, buddy. If you'll excuse me . . ." I asked him if I could send him some cigarettes, but he shook his head and said, "I got pals on the outside. They see that I get tobacco and magazines and that stuff." Then he shook hands and went back to his wild west magazines. I left the jail and went down to Police Headquarters to see Captain William J. Raftis, the head of the P.P. Squad. I wanted to ask him how Lewis rated as a pickpocket. The Captain said that Lewis was good.

"He has never been a lush roller," he said. "I mean he has never picked the pockets of drunks. He has always worked on pants pockets. Anybody could rob a drunk on the subway, or a night worker catching a nap on the way to work. Some people get into such a deep sleep on the subway you could saw their legs off. Lewis often works with a confederate, who feigns drunkenness and crowds a victim. Then Lewis picks the victim's pocket."

Captain Raftis said that most of the expert pickpockets started out quite young. Lewis began his career around 1904.

"In those days," said the Captain, "there were no compulsory education laws and kids could roam the streets and get into bad company. Also there were no laws directed specifically against pickpockets. We are not breeding many pickpockets now. My squad, and the various new laws, make it almost impossible for them to work. We have detectives working crisscross on the subway and watching all big crowds. Just as Lewis said, a pickpocket in these days is just butting his head against a wall."

2. The Pickle Works

On one side of the stage at the Alvin Theatre two tall chorus girls in rehearsal bloomers were sitting on a bench eating three-decker sandwiches and gulping light brown coffee from a cardboard container. Both girls were drinking from the same quart container, and they smudged lipstick on the rim of it every time they took a swig. They were talking with their mouths full.

An actor came in and stood beneath a sign which read: "Fire Laws Require No Smoking On Stage." Standing there, the actor took out a paper book of matches and lit a cigarette. Actors were rehearsing in every corner of the stage. Some were singing and others were yelling lines at one another. Two tapdancers stood off to one side pitching nickels at a crack in the stage. The dancer whose nickel hit nearest the crack tapped his way forward and picked up his winnings.

In the pit a piano player with a cigarette stuck in the corner of his sneering mouth and a felt hat on the back of his head was banging away. Ethel Merman stood in the middle of the stage in a big white fur coat. It was chilly on the stage. Once in a while a chorus girl would put her arms akimbo, lean forward and shiver. A rehearsal of "Red, Hot and Blue!" was in progress.

The star of the show, Jimmy Durante, sat on a shaky chair tilted against the bare bricks in the back wall of the stage. He looked as if he were trying to get as far away from other humans as possible. His face was haggard. When he took his cigar out of his big, ragged mouth his hands shook.

"I can't drink," he said, shivering. "Only my great

sense of responsibility forced me to show up at the pickle works today. I can't drink. It's all right if I take a glass of vermoot, or some red wine. Yeh, that's all right. But last night I'm feeling thirsty, so I go to this joint across the street and I say to the bartender, 'Recommend me something.' So he give me what he called an Alexander. I had about six of these here Alexanders, and I get dizzy. When I go home I hit the bed and it whirls around like an electric fan. I am sea-sick. I'm in an awful fix. I want to die.

"First time that happened in weeks and weeks. I am going on the water wagon. I'm going to sit up there with the driver, and hold on tight. That is, except for some wine with meals. Red wine, what they used to call Guinea Red, only I never liked that terminology. The French they like red wine as much as the Italians."

A chorus girl walked by, a beautiful redhead with long white arms.

"Don't believe anything he tells you," she said.

Durante jumped up and gave the girl a resound-ing smack on what might be called the hips. She squealed with laughter.

"You great big angel," said Durante, forgetting his hangover.

He got up and walked out to the orchestra, and sat down in one of the front seats, a $5.50 seat. He stuck his feet up on the seat in front. He appeared more cheerful. Two chorus girls sat in back. One was talking and the other was cracking her chewing gum.

"So he said to me, 'You're just what the doctor ordered,' " said the chorus girl. "And I said, 'Your doctor must be a dentist, you big bum, keep your hands off me.' Can you imagine. I only met him half an hour and he's trying to kiss me."

"Yeh," said her colleague, "the big bum."

"I sure do like this life," said Durante. "When I was a kid down on Catherine Street I used to have a job, delivering papers. I would grab this bundle of 500 papers, night editions, see? And I would get on the elevated and take them up to the four newsstands at Third and Fourteen Street. In those days a paper would only have twelve pages, and a kid could handle 500. Nowadays it would crush a kid if you tried to pile that many on him. It would pulverize him.

"So I take them up there. Then I rush around to the dives in the neighborhood. I would peep under them swinging wicker doors they had on the saloons, and I would see the men dancing with these dames, and drinking, and the piano player knocking the hell out of the piano, and I would think to myself, I would think, 'Geeze, if I could just get me a job in there it would be like in heaven.' I still feel the same way. The stage may be the pickle works to some people, but it's a big box of candy to me. Look at that blonde over there. Boy!"

Sitting there in the dark theater, nursing his hangover, the big-nosed comedian began to talk about his childhood, the days when he used to run wild on Catherine Street, raising hell with the other kids, the days when he liked to go barefooted and they had to run him down and catch him every winter to put shoes on him, the days when he learned that if he stuck his nose in the air and talked and kept on talking he was bound to say something funny. That is still his technique. He learned it when he lived at 90 Catherine with his brothers—Michael, who became a photoengraver, and Albert, who became a cop, both dead now. His father, robust old Bartholomeo Durante, now eighty-seven, who ran a barber shop at 87 Catherine, used to think he was nuts when he came in, talking incoherently about some experience he had in the street.

"We kids used to have a good time," he said. "They tore down where my home was and where my pop had his shop. They tore it down to put up this high-class tenement house, this Knickerbocker Village. Most of the old-timers moved out long ago. I take a walk down there sometimes at night by myself to see the mob, what's left of it. Like I drop in to see Eddie De Rosa. He runs a drugstore at 94 Catherine.

"Geeze, used to when some kid would pop me in the nose or maybe I got a nail in my foot I would rush up to Eddie's, and he would stick some iodine and court plaster on it. I go down to see Eddie, and we talk about the old days, when the East Side amounted to something.

"I went to P.S. No. 1. I quit about the sixth or seventh grade. When I was younger I would tell people I went to high school, but what's the use of bluffing? People know I'm not an educated man."

The comedian forgot all about his hangover. He said he likes to go into a pizzeria for a pizza, or rubber-pie, the big cheese and tomato pies you see in the windows of Italian restaurants. Or a dish of spaghetti with three big dippers of meat sauce. He is about as unaffected as a subway guard, and when he gets to talking about groceries nothing stops him. He will drop into a coffeepot with a copy of Variety sticking out of his coat pocket and climb up on a stool. Ten minutes later he will be telling the counterman how to run the joint.

The comedian snapped his fingers.

"Say," he said, "you should see my pop eat. He's an old man, eighty-seven. Now he lives over on Palmetto Street in Brooklyn, with my sister, Mrs. Lillian Romano, but he was with me two years in Hollywood. What a lot of laughs I get out of him!

"He loves his wine. On the way out we was eating in the diner of the train and I took this waiter aside and told him to give Pop a bottle of wine, but to take it away when he had one glass. So he does. But when he picks it up my pop made a grab for it. He jerked it out of this waiter's hand. Boy, did he grab. I nearly died laughing. This Negro waiter said, 'Mr. Jimmy said to give you some water.' Pop exploded. He said, 'Water you wash your face. Wine you wash your stomach.' Boy, did he let out a yell when he saw that wine disappearing! 'Where you go with the wine?' he yelled at this waiter.

"My pop's a barber, see? They brought him over here from Salerno, Italy, to help put up the Third Avenue El. He was just a common laborer, but he had too much sense. He saved his money and opened a barber shop. Well, he retired years and years ago, but he still carries his tools around with him, his clippers and his straight razor. He's got a mania about haircutting.

"When people come to my house he goes up and grabs at their hair and tells them they need a haircut. If they don't resist he makes them sit down right there, and he gives them a haircut. He won't take money. One day I had him on a movie set with me, and he sees Johnny Weissmuller with his long, flowing hair. Pop almost had a fit. He walks up to Johnny and says, 'What's a matter with you? Why don't you have your hair cut? Sit down and I cut it.' I had to grab him. Every morning he goes up to the priest's house in Ridgewood where he lives and shaves the priest. He won't take a dime. Just a way of amusing himself."

The comedian stood up and lit a cigar. It was raining outside. He walked to the stage door. A group of chorus girls were huddled there, waiting for the rain to slack up, so they could dash across the street to the drugstore for coffee. They had polo coats over their rehearsal clothes. Two of them were singing a song from the show.

"Look at them angels," said Durante, smacking his hands together. "Can you blame me for loving the pickle works? Why, it's a privilege to work here. I should be paying the boss for the privilege of working here. Geeze."

3. Town Anarchist Delights in Being Thought a Villain

On one of the final nights of the city's last political campaign Max Steuer made an interminable, bitter speech over WOR in which he shouted; "Why, I'll show you the kind of man La Guardia is. He associates with criminals. He associates with this man, Carlo Tresca."

When they heard these remarks many solid citizens, puzzled over which lever to pull, felt better about Fiorello La Guardia. They considered Mr. Steuer's statement a recommendation of the Fusionist.

This man, Carlo Tresca, is the town anarchist. He has lived as an exile in the United States—mostly in New York—since 1904 and is one of the city's veteran practicing political refugees. Exiled long before Mussolini came into power, he became, after 1922, a leader of the thousands of Italians exiled to the United States by the fascist dictatorship. For twelve years, a period in which strife over the Mussolini program split the Italians in this country into factions and precipitated murders and bombings and civil wars in a hundred Little Italys, Tresca has carried on a persistent campaign against the man he sometimes calls "Little Benito."

A gracious Italian, distinguished in appearance, he wears a black hat and is heavily bearded. He sometimes takes six hours for dinner and would rather be considered a villain than a hero. For many years the police believed—perhaps correctly—that he was one of the country's most dangerous men and that he frequently tossed bombs. But he is a sly anarchist.

After the bomb explosion in Wall Street in 1920, for example, his photograph was published with the caption "Police Want This Man." Members of the Bomb Squad finally located him in the People's House at 7 East Fifteenth Street, sitting in an office, sleepily reading a book on political economy. They discovered a package in his pocket. They unwrapped it and found three cheese sandwiches.

"They are nice boys," he says, referring to the Bomb Squad. "Since then, whenever there is a bomb, they come to see me. They ask me what I know, but I never know anything. So we have wine."

Now his life is comparatively placid. Years have passed since Tresca, the perennial dynamiting suspect, the antifascist, the militant editor, the I. W. W. agitator, the companion in labor struggles of sharp-tongued Elizabeth Gurley Flynn and of fat Emma Goldman, was suspected of an earth-rocking crime. Plagued by nostalgia, he sits at a restaurant table, smokes his pipe, drinks dark red wine, and recalls the headlines of other years: "Tresca Confirms Bomb Plot Aimed at Rockefeller," and "Waterbury Cops Bar Tresca Again: Arrest Companion," and "Haywood, Tresca, Miss Flynn and Two More Indicted."

He speaks often of the jails and festivals of other years. There was the Red Revel of the Anarchists in 1915. It was held in the Harlem Casino, and Emma Goldman appeared as a nun. The revel began with a waltz called "The Anarchists' Slide," which consisted of two long dips, a short slide, and what Ben Reitman, Miss Goldman's manager, styled "the eternal swing."

"Ain't it a grand sight?" Reitman is supposed to

have yelled when Miss Goldman tried vainly to essay the two dips and the slide. "Let 'er rip, Emma."

"I had a good time that night," said Tresca, who always was the idol of the lady anarchists.

And there was the time a policeman tore off Tresca's vest during a confused riot at Sixth Avenue and Forty-first Street and disclosed a romance. The vest, torn in three places, was taken to a police station. In one of the pockets the ruthless cops found a small, worn volume, "Love Sonnets" by Elizabeth Barrett Browning. A line in one poem—"And tell thy soul their roots are left in mine"—was underscored and beneath it was scribbled, "I love you, Carlo. Elizabeth Gurley Flynn, December 12, 1912." Miss Flynn, known as "The Joan of Arc of the I.W.W.," and leader of many strikes in New Jersey silk mills, was a married woman. Tresca also was married. For a time newspapers referred to them as "the trade-union lovers."

With sardonic amusement Tresca recalls another headline: "Tresca Penniless, He tells Creditors." One year ago his newspaper, Il Martello (The Hammer), in which Mussolini was soundly whacked each week, went bankrupt. Tresca's tendency to recall other days is no sign that he is slowing up. He returned that week from a trip through Italian communities in New England with Athos Terzani, the antifascist who is accused of having murdered another antifascist during a meeting in Queens of Art J. Smith's Khaki Shirts of America, a fascist organization. In December he will start publishing Il Martello again.

Tresca has three lairs. He may be found in the office, on the top floor of a loft building at 52 West Fifteenth Street, of La Stampa Libera, the nation's leading antifascist newspaper, for which he occasionally writes an essay. (This is the newspaper whose name Steuer scornfully mispronounced in his radio speech. It supported La Guardia.)

You go up to the office in a slow, grimy elevator. Most of the editors and reporters were exiled by Mussolini. They are suspicious of visitors. At noon the editors spread cheese and wine on their tables. And Tresca, if present, makes a few scurrilous remarks about Mussolini.

Tresca also puts in a daily appearance at the Manhattan office of the Industrial Workers of the World, on the third floor of 94 Fifth Avenue, one of those buildings inhabited by commercial artists, sign painters, and radical organizations. On the floor above is the office of his dormant newspaper. There is a row of benches in a hall outside the office, and scores of antifascist exiles use the room as a headquarters. Tresca listens to their tribulations, gives them good advice.

"Sure," said Tresca, "I tell you all about the exiles

from Italy. After the Fascisti took power in 1922 around 20,000 left the country, a big crowd every month, and come to the United States. For years they come. They had political beliefs very unpopular, or were Masons, or did not like any more how things looked. So they leave. The most famous, the wealthy, go to Paris or Switzerland. Great mass come here.

"Most famous to come here is Professor Gaetano Salvemini, historian and once a member of Chamber of Deputies—like a congressman here. On his way here Salvemini stops in London. There they send word his property is confiscated. He laughs. 'How funny!' he said. 'It is a compliment. All the property I have are few dry books and some sticks of furniture.' He is a respected history professor now at Yale. If he touches his foot on Italian dirt he get thirty years in jail, but maybe Mussolini would reduce the term to twenty-five. Who knows?

"Also famous was Vincenzo Vacirca. He was a deputy also. Also had his little home confiscated. Was a famous editor here one time and at present is olive oil salesman in Brooklyn. Another was Virgilia D'Andrea, most outstanding in Italian labor movement and a fine poet. She was beaten up, insulted, and her home destroyed. Only salvation was exile. Here she died a month ago.

"There were many more very famous. They are taken care of, you see, somehow, but what of the masses, the laborers and those kind of people? Not so good. Terrible. In this city there are at least 15,000 militant antifascist. All hate Mussolini very much. Positively, I know at least 3,000 are here in clandestine. They are living day by day in fear, exiles all. They change their homes two, three times a month. You see, those who live in clandestine are aliens. If they get deported, it means death in Italy. So they live in horrible fear. A racket goes on, based on fear. The fascists hunt the exiles out.

"A fascist finds an alien. All right. One night a man knocks on the door. He comes in and says, 'I am from Department of Justice. We have to deport you now.' Then he says $200 will straighten this little matter out. It is a shakedown—see? I stopped that racket three times, but up it springs again. For a time everything is quiet, and then one of my boys comes in, says they are shaking down again in the Bronx, on Staten Island, every place where Italian exiles live. It is hard for those in clandestine to get jobs. They live bad. They are unknown soldiers of antifascism.

"In Italy a man may have to go into exile if he says, 'No prosperity here. Hard times all the time.' That is called a crime against the honesty and soundness of Italian finance. Once Mussolini announce he gives amnesty to all exiles. A friend of mine, Anthony Vellucci, decides to go home. We try to talk him out, but it is no good. He believes Mussolini to tell the truth. He goes. When he gets home they arrest him and say, 'You must spend five years in prison on the island. Then everything is all right.' Nice business. Five years on that malaria island and Heaven is next stop."

Tresca delights in telling of an encounter with Mussolini in 1904.

"In Italy," he said, "I worked with socialist labor union of railroad workers. Also was editor of Il Germa [The Seed]. It is very powerful paper. Suddenly I am arrested for something I write, given sentence of eighteen months in jail or ten years in exile. So I take the exile. On my way here I stop in Basel, Switzerland. There is another exile living there. His name is Benito Mussolini. He is very weak-tempered and vain, a man who would push himself forward so people applaud. I argued all night with him. He says he is a very radical man, an extreme socialist. Next day he says goodbye to me at the station and he says, 'Tresca, you are not radical enough.'

"Can you imagine? I am an anarchist now; and what is Mussolini, who was so radical? A traitor to the cause. He remembers that incident, and if I go anywhere near Italy I don't live long."

When Tresca first came to New York he worked as editor of Il Proletario. Then he went to Pittsburgh, founded an anti-Catholic newspaper, La Plebe [The Mob]. Every Italian revolutionist is an anti-Catholic.

"Well," he said, "the churches there pulled together and started a paper to counteract mine. That is no good, so they start libel suits against me. No good either. So they send an emissary to kill me, pay him $500 in advance for job. He comes with an open razor. See this scar?"

Tresca has a broad scar which extends from a corner of his mouth to his right ear. It is very decorative.

"But I grabbed the razor. So he doesn't kill me, just slits my throat. Since they can't kill me they get the postal authorities against me. A good stunt. It succeeds. But I start another paper."

Then he left Pittsburgh, aided in the defense of Ettor and Giovannitti in Lawrence, Massachusetts, assisted in the silk-mill strikes in New Jersey and the hotel strike in New York in 1912. He led the Mesabi Range iron-ore strikes in northern Minnesota in 1916, was arrested for the murder of a deputy sheriff but never tried. During the war period, under cover, and with great difficulty, he started Il Martello. During 1917 only twenty-seven issues of the newspaper were banned.

In 1925 he was sentenced to a year in the Federal Penitentiary in Atlanta for publishing a two-line advertisement on birth control. President Calvin Coolidge cut the sentence to four months. In the Atlanta prison Tresca enjoyed himself. He collected evidence on an interprison dope ring, brought it out between the soles of his shoes. The Department of Justice begged him for the evidence, but he laughed and said, "I am only interested in tearing down your government." On his way home he stopped in Washington and followed a group of college students into the White House.

"They were on a hand-shaking expedition," he said. "So I stood in line and shook the president's hand. I wanted to say, 'Mr. Coolidge, I am the man you pardoned from the penitentiary. Thank you ever so much.' But I didn't say it. I was afraid a guard would rush up when he heard my name and yell, 'For God's sake, Mr. President, be careful. He may have a bomb in his hip pocket.' "

A few years after he left prison, the bomb period of Tresca's career came to a close. In a few weeks he will start publishing Il Martello again and his life will once again become turbulent.

3. ASCAP Investigator

In this agitated metropolis nightlife joints sprout like jimsonweeds after a spring rain.

A former coffeepot counterman with delusions of grandeur withdraws his savings and leases a vacant store, a cellar or a second-floor hall. Carpenters erect a secondhand bar with defective beer pipes and hammer some grooved boards together for a dance floor. A few cases of what are known as choice wines and liquors are toted in, and checked gingham cloths are laid on two dozen unsteady tables. The proprietor's wife buys some pots and pans and two bottles of pickled cherries and turns the kitchen over to "the chef," an unshaven ex-plumber. Miss Lucy de Lulu, an apprentice fan dancer, is hired at $12.50 a week, and an orchestra—piano, violin, saxophone and drums—is engaged. Neon signs begin to flicker and El Clippo is born.

Before the handle on the cash register is greasy an investigator from ASCAP, or the American Society of Composers, Authors and Publishers, 30 Rockefeller Plaza, hears about the establishment known as El Clippo. The moment a night spot using music sprouts up he is supposed to get on the job. He drives by at night and sees the neon signs, or he sees an advertisement.

El Clippo may be far up in the Bronx, under El tracks on Third Avenue, or in the heart of Harlem, but before many nights go by the investigator is scribbling notes on little cards. It's his job to convince the outraged proprietor that he has to get a license from ASCAP before the orchestra can legally play such artistic numbers as "It's a Sin to Tell a Lie" or "These Foolish Things (Remind Me of You)."

"It is a thorny job," said Russell W. Rome, a for-

mer Wesleyan University football player and one of
the most resourceful of ASCAP's investigators. The
majority of the backers for cabarets and dance halls in
the New York district are real tough characters. Not
all are cutthroats, of course, but you won't find many
who go to Sunday school. Some were in the liquor
racket during prohibition, and some were gangsters
or gamblers.

"When you drop in to tell them ASCAP repre-
sents the songwriters and publishers who own the
copyrights on most of the songs they play, and that
they will have to get a license from us before they can
play them legally, they usually say, 'It's a racket. Get
out of here, you bum, you sneak, you dope.'

"Making them see the light is a long, hard job.
Take a joint of the El Clippo type. We have a theo-
retical minimum of $210 a year, entitling a propri-
etor to play all our songs, but in a place like that the
rate committee would probably decide from $60 to
$90 a year would be just, depending on the capacity
of the joint, the number of hours the orchestra plays
and things like that. Some of the big swanky places
pay over $2,000 a year. We license hotels with or-
chestras, theaters, dance halls, cafés and restaurants,
radio stations, any place with an orchestra.

"When a place opens up we send a form letter
telling them what ASCAP is and asking them to apply
for a license. They throw this in the wastebasket 99

times out of 100. We wait a week and send him another notice, which also goes into the wastebasket. Then an investigator goes around. Most of those people use their bars for offices, and you stand at the bar and explain the matter. He says he didn't get the letters.

"He says he bought the sheet music, paid good money for it, and do we mean to tell him he can't make use of what he bought? We take some sheet music and show him where it says 'All rights reserved, including public performance for profit.' This does not mean a thing to him. If he is the boss he will make out he is the bartender and say, 'I got to see the boss.' Or he says he will see his lawyer or the district leader. They always have to see somebody. Then he says, 'Get out!' "

The next step is a registered letter. When it is disregarded the investigator goes to work in earnest.

"He goes up to the bar in this place and orders a beer," said Mr. Rome, "or he takes a girl along as camouflage and sits down and has a sandwich. We always drink beer or coffee. I wonder how many cups of coffee I have downed in the service of ASCAP. Sometimes I have hit as many as ten night spots a night. You have to do most of your work after midnight.

"All the investigator does is sit still and listen to the music. He writes down each title as the band plays it, and most of them are bound to be songs by our members. The band plays 'Is It True What They Say About Dixie?' That's our song. It plays 'All My Life.' That's ours.

"He writes them all down. He also writes out a description of the place so he can answer questions if he is put on the witness stand in case we finally have to bring suit. After a while he sends the waiter to the boss with his card. The boss has forgotten the matter, of course, and you have to tell him the whole damned thing again. Still he doesn't get it. He says, 'It's a racket.' You explain some more and he says, 'Get out.' Then you take your report back to the office. You have caught him in an infringement of copyright and you can bring suit."

Mr. Rome said a few more letters are dispatched. Finally the proprietor is notified that he has infringed the Copyright Law of 1909, that ASCAP has placed the matter in the hands of its attorney, that a suit will be filed in a United States District Court if he does not apply for a license.

"Now comes the headache," said Mr. Rome. "In New York City it is hard to tell who really owns a cabaret or similar place. The man they tell you owns it may turn out to be the porter. You have to get the name of the proprietor so the United States Marshal can give the subpoena to the right man. The best place to get the name is from the liquor license. We could get it through the State Liquor Authority, but it takes time. So we usually get it off the license, which is supposed to be displayed in the joint.

"Usually they hang it up where the ceiling meets the wall, where you can't possibly see it, or behind the stove in the kitchen. You have to use your wits. This is one way to get the name off the license. I go in and get in an argument with the bartender over beers. We begin to argue about eyesight. I say, 'I bet you a beer I can read the name on that license up there on the wall.' He bets, and I say any name that pops in my mind. He laughs and yells with triumph and says that isn't the name at all. I make him get the license down to prove it, and then I copy off the name.

"Another way is this: Frederick C. Erdman, the manager of the New York District, has a pair of sports binoculars in his desk. I take these glasses to a bar and say to the bartender, 'Look what I got at an auction for fifty cents.' He looks at them and focuses them here and there about the joint. Then he gets tired and I focus them here and there, finally concentrating on the license. You can usually read them that way."

"When we get the name the Marshal goes around to serve the subpoena, and an investigator goes along to point out the boss. I remember one night at a tough little joint full of sailors, Filipinos and their girls in the Brooklyn Navy Yard district. The boss has already told me, 'Buddy, if you ever put your face in here again I'll smack it through the wall.' I believed the gentleman would do it, so I let the Marshal talk.

"He handed him the paper. The boss tore it up and knocked the Marshal flat on his back. I picked up the pieces and handed them to the boss and ran for the door. I usually keep between the proprietor and the door. This is a good policy. The Marshal got cops, and finally the boss got nicer and decided to apply for a license. He even bought a round of drinks."

After a subpoena is served most proprietors see their lawyers and finally realize that they must apply and pay for a license. It takes them a long time to understand that music is not free. If he takes it to court the probable damages he will have to pay is $250 for each infringement, and each time a song is played constitutes a separate infringement. Few cases end in court. Before a contentious proprietor is permitted to take out a license he has to pay the Marshal's charge and other court costs.

There are nine investigators in the New York Office. All understand the sixes and sevens of popular music, and most are college graduates. ASCAP maintains offices in key cities throughout the country, and investigators work out of them. If a beer hall with music opened in Ashpole, North Carolina, or if a hotel engages an orchestra in Claremont, Texas, ASCAP investigators will be around before the bar is thoroughly seasoned with alcohol.

"We are selling an intangible," said Mr. Rome, "and it is hard to make people realize it isn't a racket and that songwriters are entitled to receive real money for songs. They are buying something they can't eat, something they can't hold in their hands, and they consider it a strange bill of goods."

4. SALTWATER FARMERS

I

Into a section of blue, shallow water in Great South Bay, marked off by four poles, Captain Jacobus Kwaak steered his old copper-sheathed Willie K., flagship of the Bluepoint oyster fleet. When he reached the middle of the bed the Captain slowed down, and two oystermen in hip boots ran forward and dropped the starboard dredge. The heavy dredge bumped over the bottom, stripping bushels of fat, five-year-old oysters from their resting places.

In a few minutes the dredge was pulled up and its sloshing load dumped on the deck. With the oysters the dredge always brings up an allowance of trash, and this time it brought up a number of baby crabs, several handfuls of sea lettuce, an ugly toadfish, a scattering of sea snails, a starfish and three bunches of dirty sponge. The old Captain yelled for one of his men to take the wheel. Then, grunting, he climbed to the deck and bent over the heap of dripping oysters. He threw a handful of trash overboard, dug into the pile and selected an oyster, a big one.

He drew a rusty old knife and opened the oyster. It lay in its left shell, clean and fat. With the blade of the knife he tapped the narrow end of the oyster, the fat end which holds the stomach, the digestive sacs and the heart. The fat bulged under the strokes of the blade. Through with his inspection, Captain Kwaak lifted the shell into the air and expertly dropped the oyster into his mouth.

"This will be a good oyster year," he said. "The whole crop is good. We had enough rough weather to roil up the water on the bottom of the beds, stirring up the microscopic vegetable matter the oysters feed on. They are fat, salty-tasting and thrifty. Their parasites, the starfish and the drill-snail, haven't been loose in the beds. The oysters are as good as I ever tasted and I've been eating at least a dozen a day for sixty-five years."

The oyster syndicate for which the Captain works, the Bluepoints Company, Inc., a subsidiary of General Foods Corporation, will dredge up and ship this season approximately 100,000 barrels of oysters in shells and around 300,000 gallons of shucked oysters in cans. It and its subsidiaries, oyster farms in Connecticut, Rhode Island and Long Island, have approximately 5,000,000 bushels of oysters of varying ages lying on the bottoms of Great South and other shallow bays.

There will be a bumper crop this year. In the Long Island area alone the yield this year for all oyster companies, syndicated and independents, will total more than 1,500,000 bushels. This week the business will get under way in earnest after four warm spawning months, and along the Atlantic seaboard, on the finest oyster farms in the world, around 25,000 men are back at work, hauling oysters out of the beds, shoveling them into barrels, culling them into many sizes and qualities, throwing them into conditioning basins, shucking them for long shipments.

The tap of the hammers wielded by the graders can be heard in hundreds of sheds in Long Island, and in immaculate but smelly barns, rows of shuckers, largely hearty men of Dutch descent or Negroes from the beds of Virginia and Maryland, are shucking thousands of oysters every day. They will work feverishly until next May.

Most of the oysters you will eat this winter were planted at least five years ago. The similarities between oyster-growing and truck-farming are close. Like tomatoes, oysters are first planted in seed beds, then weeded out and transplanted. In fact, in the three to five years it takes to mature seed oysters to a size fit for marketing, they may be transplanted three or four times. An immobile oyster may be born off Rhode Island, transplanted to beds in Connecticut and spend the last two years of its life in Long Island.

"All this transplantation and the fight oyster-men have to carry on against parasites are what make oysters cost so much more than they should," said Joseph B. Glancy, an official of the Bluepoints Company, who has done research in oyster-farming up and down the Atlantic coast for ten years.

"An enormous amount of capital is tied up in the business. For example, the company I work for owns, through riparian laws, a total of 14,000 acres of bay bottom, and of this only about 3,000 acres are suitable for oyster beds. If the bottom is too muddy, it is no good for oysters because they get lost in it and suffocate, and a loose, shifting, sandy bottom is no good because your oysters may be swept by a storm over into beds owned by another company.

"All our beds are staked out and mapped, of course. We have thirty boats varying in capacity from 500 to 4,500 bushels of oysters, and the captains know the beds. Captain Kwaak knows the bottom of Great South Bay as well as a farmer knows his fields. He watches over them all the time, and when the season opens he goes from bed to bed, dredging up a few bushels here and a few more there, sampling them to see if they are ready for marketing, watching out for starfish and drills.

"You saw dredgers on the Willie K. haul up a few bushels out of bed No. 21 a while ago and the Captain found them all right. When he goes back to the plant he will say the oysters there are ready to go and his boat and the other boats will start bringing them in by the hundreds of bushels. All the oysters out there in Great South Bay may be called Bluepoints if they have been left there at least three months. According to a New York State law an oyster must spend that time in the bay before it may legally be called a Bluepoint."

Captain Kwaak's sturdy boats leave the marketing beds (beds in which oysters feed from six months to two years before they are brought in) and make fast to a wharf beside the Bluepoint Company's sheds at West Sayville, Long Island. The oysters are hoisted from the boat to a loft and then dropped into a row of bins. Standing at these bins are men in boots with burlap sacks wrapped around their legs who tap each oyster with a hammer to see that it is sound. Then, they grade them, throwing them into one of a half-circle of barrels.

There are many grades. The Bluepoint is a small, round oyster which will run 1,300 to a barrel. There is a type called the half-shell size, which runs 1,000 to the barrel. Mediums are oysters suitable for frying and too large to eat on the half-shell, which run 750 to the barrel and may be sold as Cape Cods. The Rockaway or Lynnhaven is the granddaddy. Only 500 may be crammed into the iced barrels.

Mr. Glancy said the oystermen kept a close watch on their beds, but that they were bothered often by poachers.

"There are millions of dollars worth of oysters lying out there on the bottom of the bay," he said, "and stealing is inevitable. On foggy nights the thieves run out there and play havoc. Sometimes they have a little motorboat and take the oysters with tongs, and sometimes they have dredges on their boats.

"There is no way to eradicate them. About the only man who was able to keep them off his beds was Stanley Lowndes, the millionaire oysterman, who weighed 400 pounds. He's dead now.

"He was having a lot of trouble with stealing in the fattening grounds on Staten Island, which used to be perfect for oysters. One day he went out to his beds and caught a boat red-handed. The thieves were loading them on as if they owned the place. Mr. Lowndes was very angry.

"He pulled up alongside the thief's boat and tied up to it. 'You want oysters, do you?' he yelled at the thief. Well, he had a mountain of oysters on his own boat and he put his men to work dumping them on the thief's boat. Pretty soon it sank to the bottom of the bay. The thief and his men had to swim ashore. Mr. Lowndes followed them in with his boat and now and then he'd yell, 'I'm keeping your boat for evidence.' He didn't have much more trouble with pirates."

II

The hale, thrifty Long Islanders with Dutch names and capacious stomachs who plant and harvest the oyster crops combine the techniques of the seaman, the biologist and the farmer. Captain Jacobus Kwaak is a representative oysterman, who smokes one of the strongest black briar pipes in the Western hemisphere and stamps about the deck of his oyster boat in all weather with the vigor of a man of forty, although he is approaching seventy-five, a condition he explains by his habit of eating anywhere from a dozen to a bushel of oysters a day for sixty-five years.

The Captain came from Zeeland, the Netherlands, when he was three. After attending a school on Long Island for nine months he decided he was an educated man and got a job in the oyster sheds. He has worked with oysters ever since, becoming an authority on their habits, habits which have puzzled generations of biologists. At intervals he has reared ten children. He has also become one of the most respected citizens in his hometown, West Sayville, and one of the best amateur weather prophets in America, basing his predictions on the way the oysters feed and the manner in which they bed. He consumes with gusto a large portion of each oyster crop harvested on the Atlantic seaboard, and when he goes to a restaurant and sees people ordering fruit cups and tomato juice instead of oysters, the sight bewilders him, causes him to believe that someone forgot to lock the doors of the asylums.

"In the summer months, the months without an R in their names, the oysters spawn. That is the reason we don't encourage the eating of oysters during those months. They won't hurt you, but just before they spawn they have a flat taste and just after they are thin and stringy. I can't look at an oyster and tell if it's a male or a female. Most oysters start as males and some change to females in later years. We can be sure, though, that the ratio of sexes in a spawning bed is about 50–50.

"When the water gets warm enough the female oyster throws out from ten to sixty million microscopic eggs, and the male throws out sperm. They float together in the water and form larvae, which float or lie on the bottom for two weeks. Then they attach themselves to the 'clutch,' the old oyster shells we threw overboard. In a few months we can pull them up and figure out just about what our crop will be five years from then. It takes them five years to develop.

"A bunch of little oysters will stick to one old shell, and we have to knock them off and spread them out, giving them room to grow, just like a farmer with a crop of corn. Also, the time a farmer spends weeding his corn we have to spend weeding out the starfish and the drills, the two oyster parasites."

Captain Kwaak and other oyster captains spend a period of each year eradicating the starfish. This animal wraps itself affectionately around an oyster and pries open its shell. Then it deposits its own stomach in the oyster's shell, covers the oyster with gastric juices, eats it and then recovers its freewheeling stomach.

Once an official of the Bluepoints Company, the largest oyster company in the world, for which Captain Kwaak works as commander of the flagship, Willie K., heard an oyster shucker ask the Captain what was the most oysters he ever ate at one sitting.

"One night me and a friend sat down and ate a barrel of half-shells," said the Captain. (There are approximately 1,000 half-shells in a barrel.)

"Well, Captain, I guess you didn't eat much supper that night, did you?" asked the oyster shucker.

"Hell," said the Captain, "that was right after supper."

According to his mood, the Captain thinks of himself as a farmer or as a biologist.

"We farm under water," he said, "and we have to prepare our ground just like a truck-farmer. To get the bottoms out in the bay ready for planting we drop tons of old oyster shells overboard. We throw at least 500 bushels of old shells to each acre of bottom. We call the shells 'clutch.' The little oysters attach themselves to the old shells."

The oystermen mop the bottoms of their beds with long cotton mops in their struggle against the starfish. The parasite gets tangled in the mop and is brought to the deck. There it is quickly doused with boiling water. It is an expensive process, and if you think oysters should be cheaper you should hate the starfish.

Spread out on the bottom of Great South Bay, which has an average depth of nine feet, the oysters strain gallons of salt water through their gills and eat microscopic vegetables and animals, gorging on the larvae of snails and clams. A cannibal, the oyster also eats its own larvae. Most oystermen boast with justice that oysters are one of the most healthful foods in the world. The biologists employed by the industry have found that oysters are high in protein, rich in iodine and mineral salts, especially so with respect to iron, copper and manganese. If you are bothered by such matters, it may please you to know that the oyster possesses "well-balanced nutritional potencies of Vitamins A, B, C and D." It also bears Vitamin G, which fights against pellagra.

Most oystermen eat oysters raw with no sauce. The only workers in the industry who lack tremendous enthusiasm for oysters as food are the shuckers, the men who stand at bins all day and open oysters for shipment in cans. Few of them will eat more than a dozen a day.

The shuckers are skilled workmen. A beginner is apt to cut both hands off attempting to open an oyster. There are two methods of shucking. One is the cracking method, in which the worker knocks off the tip of the shell, inserts his knife and forces the shells apart. The other method, known as "side-knifing," is simpler, but it requires thick muscles. The worker simply takes the oyster in an iron grip, inserts the knife and tears the shells apart with a twist of his wrist.

The sheds in which oysters are shucked, washed and canned are immaculate. All utensils are sterilized, and the benches at which shuckers work are hosed over each night with live steam. The shuckers are paid on a piecework basis. The present rate is 25 cents a gallon. The highest any man made last year was $11 for a day's work in which he shucked 44 gallons, or 8,800 oysters.

Captain Kwaak believes oysters should be eaten right out of their shells. "A sauce is not worth the bother," he said. "Some dry cracker tastes good with an oyster sometimes, but horseradishes and such stuff is no good. The best way to eat oysters, of course, is out at the beds. I have to restrain myself when I am hauling them in. When we are dredging, the pile on the deck grows until it is level with my wheelhouse. When it gets that high, I reach out and start eating.

"I have made it a practice to eat oysters or clams every day of my life, and now they are almost as necessary as water. This summer I drove out to Denver to see one of my seven daughters, and I wanted some clams. I went into a Denver restaurant and they had six cherrystones on the menu for one buck. I told the waiter I'd starve to death before I'd pay that much for a half-dozen clams."

East Coast oystermen are contemptuous of Pacific oysters, finding them bitter and unpalatable and often from Japanese seed. They respect the famous Colchester oysters of England and the green Marennes oysters of France, and they are proud that Europeans have developed such a taste for oysters from the eastern coast of the United States that thousands of barrels are shipped abroad each year. However, many Great South Bay oystermen believe that by far the best oyster in the world is a well-nourished fat Bluepoint or Cape Cod from Mattituck Creek in Great Poconic Bay.

"You can search all the waters in the world," said Captain Kwaak, selecting a Bluepoint from the heap level with his wheelhouse window, "and you won't find better seafood than oysters from Long Island Sound."

5. New Cycle in Comic Art

Peter Arno

"I don't think anything could be so much fun as to get a good hold on a pompous person and shake him or her until you can hear the false teeth rattling," said Peter Arno, who has made the pompous, big-bosomed mama a symbol of a withering social order.

It was late in the afternoon and the well-tailored cartoonist had just turned up at his disheveled studio, an entire floor at 15 East Fifty-sixth Street. While he talked, he chewed hungrily on a Virginia ham sandwich and drank from a paper container of coffee, his breakfast.

The floor around his drawing board was covered with charcoal sketches made late at night and tossed aside for revision—sketches made with the utmost care, but looking as if they were scratched off in a moment or two.

Stacked in a corner of the big room were three wooden cases stamped "Berry Bros., & Co., Wine

Merchants." "I have ten more cases in Nassau. Swell old rye. Picked it up at thirty-five a case because they didn't know how good it was themselves. Already they're trying to buy it back at eighty a case. No sale."

Talking, the cartoonist jumped nervously from subject to subject. There was a telephone at his elbow, and it went off every few minutes. He would jump to his feet to answer it, stamping his shoes against the floor in a tentative tapdance as he talked.

"At no time in the history of the world," he said, sloshing his coffee about in the pasteboard container, "have there been so many damned morons together in one place as here in New York right now. Any night in the big night clubs. The town squirms with them. Vain little girls with more alcohol in their brains than sense. Take a look in any night club, or the fancy restaurants around lunchtime.

"The kind of person with money who sits and says to himself, 'I'm hot stuff; I'm just about the hottest stuff around.' Pompous. The fat old guy snorting around town as if he owned the earth and all that's on it. The wheezy old dowager sitting up in her opera box with a frown on her fat face . . ."

The telephone rang again, urgently. A friend called to give him advice about a traffic violation involving an appearance in court.

It appears that Mr. Arno is still fond of extracting speed from gasoline and has not changed in this respect from the days when he complained to the Packard Motor Car Company that his automobile was not capable of 100 miles per hour. Now he drives a Duesenberg, a slick job. He had a lot of fun at the Vanderbilt Cup Race at Westbury; among his friends are some of the best speed drivers in the country.

"Yes," he said, tossing the telephone into its trough, "those people make me mad, the young ones more than the old ones. You don't do good work of this sort unless you're mad at something. I'm sure that's true. For several years I wasn't mad at anything. I went to Hollywood and fooled around. My work suffered. My work wasn't worth a damn.

"I've always rebelled against the social order, if you get what I mean. At least, against some aspects of it. As I grew up, it became dissatisfaction with the life around me. I would see fatuous, ridiculous people in public places, in night clubs where I ran a band, on trains and beaches, in cafés, at parties, and I was awfully annoyed by them, by the things they did and said. I had a really hot impulse to go and exaggerate their ridiculous aspects. That anger, if you like, gave my stuff punch and made it live. I mean, I don't know anything better to call it than anger."

"Why were you angry?" he was asked. "You have always been as well-fed as the people you caricature. You led a successful jazz band. One of your shows

["The New Yorkers," in 1930, with the violent Clayton, Jackson and Durante, amiable Frances Williams, and Ann Pennington, with the classy legs] was one of the best revues ever produced in the United States. You have been a successful cartoonist from the start. So what kept you from becoming complacent and fat-faced?"

"Oh, hell, I don't know," said Mr. Arno, balling up the sheet of waxed paper in which his sandwich had been wrapped and tossing it into the air. "What's gained by making generalities about yourself?"

The cartoonist was quiet for ten minutes or so, thinking the matter over. He decided that, as much as anything else, his contempt for the self-satisfied and the fatuous was generated by his interest in the Civil War period and by his respect for the drawings by Honoré Daumier, which he found in books in the library of his father, the late Supreme Court Justice Curtis A. Peters.

Arno was fascinated by Daumier, who worked on the staffs of magazines similar to The New Yorker, La Caricature, and Charivari, who was put in jail for six months for a cartoon of Louis Philippe as Gargantua, who died in 1879, a blind old man, leaving at least 3,958 lithographs for a grateful posterity.

Arno's interest in the Civil War had its effect. Although he seldom talks about it, he is a fair student of the war. He has a collection of biographies and histories and his hero is General Nathan Bedford Forrest, who captured 31,000 prisoners. (He is partisan, holding out for the South, although his father's people were New Englanders and his mother was English.)

The point is that he was impressed by "the grace and the decency and the customs of the civilization of the South," and he used what he read about that civilization as a basis of comparison when he observed his contemporaries. It was, of course, an unjust comparison. However, he found his contemporaries lacking.

The piercing lithographs of Daumier, then, and an interest in the Civil War, and the fact that he grew up when reputations of hundreds of idols were being deflated, caused Arno to look upon what was once considered "a sweet old lady" and decide she was a "fat-faced old mama, who grunts when she sits down," and to look upon a snorting general, with a few score pounds of badges pinned to his coat, as a comic figure. That is his own analysis.

Now thirty-three, Arno has seen his draftsmanship and outlook influence most of his contemporaries in the field of the humorous drawing. He is by no means satisfied with his work. He quit drawing the Whoops Sisters, a pair of raucous, uninhibited ladies he originated in 1926, because he was afraid the customers were beginning to find them hackneyed. Lately he purchased a candid camera, a device found valuable by other cartoonists. He develops his own films, does his own enlargements.

"I think of my drawing as reporting," he said, "and I think I'm approaching a truer and sounder style of reporting. I like the people in my drawings to have the startled looks on their faces you sometimes see in the flashlight photo. I take a lot of candid shots and use them as memos. I take them under theater marquees, in night clubs, on Fifth Avenue late in the afternoon and places like that. I get a lot of tips from them.

"I take photographs when I am on vacation at Martha's Vineyard, or in the Bahamas, and I have done some posed stuff under studio lights. I've also got some pretty good pictures in airplanes.

"I think I am changing as an artist, but I can't explain how. More and more I'm getting to keep regular hours. I've led a pretty quiet life the last year or so. However, a cartoonist can't sit in his hole. I have to get around at night to new places to see strange-looking people. I'm sure I've never used any one person for a character. I'll see maybe twenty or thirty persons of one type and I'll get a little something I can use from all of them.

"I don't like to draw young people. I don't think they're funny. Most humorous situations to me involve older people. There is some salt in what they do or say. Young people lack experience, and what they say is more pathetic to me than funny. It's the old bird sitting in a club window day in and day out that I like to draw, or types of white-mustached colonels, or the rather timid husband of the beautiful wife, the little man with drooping mustaches and childlike eyes.

"I like to work late at night. Of course, I sometimes work during the day, but I like to get in here after dinner, when things have quieted down and I can concentrate. Or sometimes I come up here to my studio after a show, around midnight, and I'll get lost in my work and stay here at the drawing board until five or six in the morning. Sometimes I drink coffee to keep going. I don't do so much drinking any more, and I wish the legend of me as a hell-raiser would die."

Arno is a prolific cartoonist. He has turned out five books of cartoons. He said The New Yorker gets first refusal on his cartoons and he is under contract to deliver a minimum of forty drawings a year. He does advertising drawings, working directly for agencies, and he does a two-page feature once a month for College Humor. He does a stack of rough sketches for magazines and finishes them after the editors have made their selections. He said that 80 percent of the gags are his own, but he uses ideas he gets from editors, or ideas that come in the mail.

He has no interest in political cartoons; he is too little interested in politicians to find them funny. Someone connected with the Democratic Campaign Committee asked for and was refused permission to use one of his drawings, a picture of some typical Arno citizens with the gag-line "Let's go to the Trans-Lux and hiss Roosevelt." He didn't register because he didn't want particularly to vote for Roosevelt and he considered Landon "a pathetic little puppet."

However, he was pleased when Heywood Broun called him "the most effective proletarian artist now functioning in America." Mr. Broun decided, "The Daily Worker is fond of using the prefix 'Mr. Fullbelly' when it mentions the various industrial leaders whom it hates. Arno does the same thing rather more concisely with a curved line."

He is proud that his formal education as an artist was exceedingly limited. "Oh, I went to the Yale Art School for a month and walked out in disgust," he said. "Then I went to the Art Students' League for a month and walked out. My teachers were just as disgusted. They tried to iron out of me the very thing that means something in my work. I painted some conventional still lifes just to show them what I could do at Yale.

"This may sound like bragging, but they stood behind me and watched me work one day, and one teacher said the thing I turned out was the kind of thing George Luks would have done. Then I did another one in broken colors and they compared it with a Monet. It's on permanent exhibition at the Yale Art School."

The cartoonist appeared to be pleased by this recollection. "I showed them what I could do," he said.

Helen Hokinson

The funniest people in the republic to Helen E. Hokinson, formerly of Mendota, Illinois, and daughter of a salesman for the Moline Plow Company, are the middle-aged ladies who live in exclusive Westchester towns, in the Oranges or in the Gramercy Square neighborhood, and whose more or less empty lives revolve in a dignified fashion around the garden or culture club, the beauty shop and the detective story.

They are women who have charge accounts, plenty of leisure, poodle dogs, chauffeurs, a box at the opera and the right to sit in Gramercy Park. They have regular appointments with hairdressers, and the hard cash some of them spend in beauty shops would wreck a bank.

Their husbands are executives and brokers. They are on the boards of private charities, and there are a flock of Madame Presidents among them.

Just about all their activities are funny to Miss Hokinson, perhaps the best lady cartoonist in America, who has a sharp eye, a dry sense of humor and plenty of ability with charcoal and wash.

Her work is personal and feminine. She deals almost entirely with females, and she can rip a woman apart, but when she goes to work on a man she merely scratches him. As a matter of fact, Dorothy McKay is about the only one of the women cartoonists whose work does not always show "the woman angle."

The boudoir and the fitting room in a fashionable shop and the parlor are the scene of most cartoons by Barbara Shermund, Alice Harvey and Mary Petty, Miss Hokinson's colleagues.

Miss Petty, for example, is typified by a cartoon showing a spectacled dame in an evening gown with a train. The saleswoman beside her says, "I want Miss Moak to look at you, Ma'am. Miss Moak is our trouble-shooter."

Miss Shermund draws giddy, angular girls. For example, two girls are lounging about in a room, one in pajamas and one in an evening dress. The latter says, "I told him there are some things I won't do, and going to a museum is one of them."

Miss Hokinson goes farther afield for her characters.

"I see my women at the flower show, the dog show and places like that," she said. "I find them at concerts, trying their best to be moved by the music, because it is so cultured. And I see them at flower shows talking about flowers and giving their Latin names, which amuses me because I have a nice flower garden and I like flowers as well as they do, but I don't know a single Latin name.

"I don't like people to get the idea I am bitter about them. I just think they're funny. I seldom draw the vicious type—they don't interest me at all. The ones who are unconsciously funny are the ones I like."

Her cartoons emphasize the frivolous in the clubwoman type. There is her fat hostess in a room full of women who guides another fat lady up to a group and says, "Mrs. Purvis is just back from Spain. She says they're wearing their skirts QUITE short."

There are the two middle-aged ladies—whether Miss Hokinson's ladies are "middle-aged" or "elderly" is puzzling—who are coming down the steps from a shabby apartment house. In one window is a sign, "Mrs. Digby, the Spiritualist, Messages." Both the ladies look vaguely disappointed. One turns to the other and says, "Someday I'm going to a *five*-dollar medium."

Many of the situations she satirizes take place in beauty shops or fashionable stores, and a frequent character is the fatuous saleswoman, anxious to make a sale and to impress the customer with her taste. She is the one who says to the clubwoman standing before the looking glass, "If it gives Madame a stomach we can take it out."

"One time a newspaper man in Boston wrote me a letter and said he rather liked my clubwomen drawings, but that for a long time he didn't really believe they existed," said Miss Hokinson. "But he enclosed a clipping from a rotogravure section showing a meeting of clubwomen, and it was exactly like one of my uplift-club cartoons."

One of her best club-meeting cartoons is one in which Edna St. Vincent Millay is sitting on the platform (it is a good caricature of Miss Millay). One old sister jumps up impulsively and, waving her hand, says, "Madame President, I move we read some of our poems for Miss Millay after she finishes."

Miss Hokinson spends most of the year in a bungalow she calls Columbine Cottage, on Dishpan Creek in Silvermine, Connecticut. It is a section in which many artists have settled. She works in a little frame house which is mostly windows built in the woods at the edge of a meadow. She can look up from her drawing board and see an overfed horse named Charley grazing on the thick Connecticut grass and switching his tail at the flies. Beside her drawing board she keeps a filing cabinet in which she has laid away hundreds of sketches.

In the files are sketches made on concert programs, on envelopes, on the margins of newspapers, on the insides of paper-match folders.

"People from all over send me ideas for cartoons," she said. "I give them a commission if I use the idea. There is a lady over in New Jersey who sends me a lot. I've never seen her. If she hears a saleswoman say something funny, she sends it to me. I like to get them."

Miss Hokinson also finds types for her cartoons at church suppers and bingo parties in the community in which she lives.

An old man runs a sawmill across Silvermine River from her bungalow, and she buys church-supper tickets from his wife.

Miss Hokinson's real name is Haakonson. Her father was Swedish, but he Americanized the name soon after settling in Illinois. She left Mendota to study at the Academy of Fine Arts in Chicago, planning to be a fashion artist.

"I wanted to earn my living," she said. "I didn't

want to go back to Mendota, although it's a nice place. My mother still lives in Sterling, Illinois, and I go out there every Christmas."

After studying at the Academy, she stayed in Chicago for two years, doing fashion drawings for Marshall Field's and other stores. Then she came to New York City; she thinks "it was somewhere around 1922, because I was here a couple of years before The New Yorker started."

She was a routine fashion artist for several years. At one time in this period she did a comic strip for a tabloid and called it Sylvia in the Big City.

"It was terrible," she said. "One of the editors came over to me and said, 'Now, listen. Your audience is composed of the gum-chewers and you got to appeal to them.' I lasted five or six months, but in that time I saved enough money so I could look around for a while."

The turning point in her career was the discovery of the theory of dynamic symmetry, which states that there is geometric form to everything— a snowflake, a leaf, the human body—and that the artist should "organize on his drawing surface a series of similar shapes based in symmetrical triangulation, and the picture will grow in conformity with nature's plan."

The theory is not generally accepted, but some of

the best artists who ever lived, including George Bellows, believed in it, and it worked out fine for Miss Hokinson.

"I found out about dynamic symmetry in a night class taught by Howard Giles at the Parsons School," she said. "It changed me entirely. When I am drawing now, sketching a person unawares even, I start with little rough triangular shapes and work out from that.

"It is wonderful for catching the gestures of people or the way they wear their hats or coats.

"Mr. Giles told us to sit in the subway on our way to class and draw people, how they were sitting, in straight lines—no curves at all. I would draw pictures of women with these straight lines and Mr. Giles would look at them and laugh. I was hurt. He said to keep at it.

"One day Garrett Price saw some drawings I made on a deck when I was seeing a friend off. They were just pictures of fat women waving to friends, fluttering their handkerchiefs.

"He said I should take them to The New Yorker, which was then a new magazine. I did, and they took them, and I've been drawing for them ever since. At first my cartoons were printed with no captions. Then they began putting captions on them, and after a while I got the knack.

"I prefer no captions on most cartoons. I think it would be just as well if the cartoon told the whole story. Of course, I'd rather have a caption when it's something like, 'If it gives Madame a stomach we can take it out!' "

William Steig

Not yet thirty, William Steig sold his first cartoon in 1930 and has become in six years one of the most respected humorous artists in the country, celebrated as much for his draftsmanship as for the comedy and social criticism inherent in his pictures of middle-class married life, of humans eating and drinking, of city children. He is perhaps best known for his cartoons of kids, the series of Small Fry cartoons.

He became a successful cartoonist with a minimum of backing and filling. After two years at the College of the City of New York, where he was a water polo star, he decided he wanted to be an artist. He talked the matter over with his father, Joseph Steig, then a house-painting contractor, but now a painter of crowd scenes, and they came to the conclusion it would be wise for him to study at the National Academy of Design.

After leaving the Academy he found that cartoons were what he wanted to draw all the time and he has concentrated on cartoons, although he is a good watercolor artist and one of his watercolors, "The Protest"—a study of a husband and wife—now hangs in the Brooklyn Museum.

"I had to break away from the things I learned at the Academy," he said. "You develop nothing but bad habits in places like that. I had a good time there. We played football in the backyard during lunch hours and we used to hang out in an ice-cream parlor near the school and talk about art.

"The people were nice there, but I had to break away from the training I got. I imagine most cartoonists who went to formal art schools had the same experience. I am satisfied to do humorous drawings. I think the cartoon is a worthy art."

Many of Mr. Steig's cartoons and cover designs, particularly those of wide-eyed city kids, are based on memories of his experiences in the streets and in vacant-lot baseball and football fields of upper Manhattan, where he was born, and the Bronx, to which he moved when he was a child. Many of the kids in the Small Fry series probably went to P.S. 53 with him.

His Small Fry drawings are more realistic and reflect a higher regard for children than the glossy, varnished paintings by women in the women's magazines.

There is the frightened little girl with her tiny hands clasped tightly together who looks through the window at the lightning in the sky; there is the boy who has found a worm in his apple; and there is the puzzled boy who laboriously has taken an alarm clock apart.

Perhaps you remember his drawing of a pleased small boy who has piled four pillows on a couch and is lolling on them while he demolishes a big lollipop. The title is "Sensualist."

Mr. Steig is an urban cartoonist. All his people live in apartments or tenement flats. When he draws a country cartoon, it is a cartoon about city people on a farm in Connecticut for the summer. He lives at least six months of the year in Connecticut. His Colonial-style house is near the town of Sherman, but he gets his mail at Gaylordsville, his telephone exchange is New Milford, and the train he sometimes uses to get home after his weekly trip to Manhattan stops at Brewster, New York. Consequently, he does not quite know how to tell people where he lives.

He comes from an unusual family. Ten years ago there wasn't an artist in the family and now there are eight. His father, who came here thirty years ago from Lemberg, a town then in Austria, but now in Poland, was a house-painting contractor until 1932, when illness caused him to retire. Since then he has been painting. He has held one exhibition.

"He paints crowds," said his son. "Such things as state fairs and band concerts. I don't think he's painted a picture that didn't have at least 100 persons in it.

"My mother, Loura Steig, started painting last February and she is very good. I guess you would call her a primitive. My wife, Elizabeth Mead, is an artist. She does baroque interiors. My brother Henry is an artist. He is also a writer. Right now he is doing some stories on swing musicians, under the name of Henry Anton. His wife, Mimi Steig, is a genre painter. My other brother, Arthur, writes advertising copy for an agency, but he is also a painter. He is the best artist in the family. His wife, Phyllis Steig, paints people. Sometime soon we are all going to hold an exhibition together."

Since his marriage last January, Mr. Steig has quit making cartoons satirizing domestic situations. He did not quit, however, because a few months of married life convinced him that his drawings of the bored husband in the overstuffed chair were untrue or unfunny, but for the same reason that Peter Arno quit drawing the Whoops Sisters—he wanted to stop before the public got tired of them.

He likes best to draw pictures of persons engaged in actions which show exactly what kind of humans they are—eating corn on the cob, for example, or sitting around the house after dinner, reading the paper. Some of his best work is in two series of character studies of persons eating and drinking he made for Vanity Fair. There is the buttermilk drinker, a fat-faced man with carefully parted hair; and there is the beer drinker, a stout gentleman with a ragged mustache and a pleased expression.

In his drawing of eaters, he really appears to be enjoying himself. There you see what he calls "the pseudo-correct eater," a double-chinned lady who holds both little fingers outstretched as she fatuously drinks tea and eats a biscuit; and "the beast," a gentleman who grasps a huge poppy-seed roll in one hand and a spoon of hot soup in the other.

Mr. Steig's mind is inquisitive and he has tried to figure out for his own satisfaction just why people laugh at cartoons. He does not believe that laughter, even that precipitated by a cartoon, is always noble, finding that "quite often there is a certain amount of viciousness in it."

"I think that laughter over a cartoon or a comic strip is pretty well explained by a man named A. M. Ludovici, who wrote a book called 'The Secret of Laughter,' " he said. "A lot of cartoonists believe he is right. He calls his idea 'the theory of superior adaptation.' The idea is that a thing is funny if it creates in the spectator a feeling of superior adaptation, that for the moment he is a superior person, certainly superior to the man who has been hit over the head with a rolling pin.

"Take for example a man who understands a foreign language. He hears someone trying to say something in this language and he thinks the mispronunciations are exceedingly funny. He feels superior.

"It is easy to laugh at cartoons of kids, because we are certainly better adapted than they are. At the same time kids are delighted at a chance to laugh at a grown-up. The more ridiculous an adult is in a slap-stick comic strip, the more they laugh. At the same time kids like pictures of other kids. I've seen children laughing at my Small Fry drawings and they undoubtedly felt superior.

"I think that a sense of humor can be carried too far. For example, there are speakers who realize that the only way they can put something over is to tell a lot of anecdotes. Audiences feel that if a speaker isn't funny he's no good, and that is bad.

"Enjoyment of a cartoon also involves what Freud calls release of psychic tension. We are all inhibited and a piece of humor breaks down these inhibitions. A nonsense drawing releases one momentarily from the burden of serious thinking."

Mr. Steig believes the cartoonist is an important citizen in periods when the world is afflicted with depressions and the growing-pains concomitant with changes in the social order. People are bewildered by the times and they turn to cartoons, just as they turn to moving pictures and jazz music, for a release, for an opportunity to laugh and feel superior.

He is glad that cartoonists have quit depending on he-said and she-said jokes, but he believes that the dependence on gag-lines likely will become as bore-some. He believes that a drawing which can take any one of six different gag-lines likely will be a bad humorous drawing, and he looks forward to a period when most cartoons will have no titles or gags beneath them at all. Unlike many cartoonists, he writes his own captions.

He is a prolific cartoonist, and he works with no soul-heaving. He works with pen and ink, with wash, with charcoal and with watercolors. He does cover designs in gouache, which is more opaque than the usual watercolors. For amusement he works on his thirty-acre farm, pruning apple trees or working about in his flower garden. Also for amusement, he carves figures out of wood cut from fruit trees.

"I've been carving wood for about a year and I find a lot of pleasure in it," he said. "We cut down some fruit trees out here and I use the wood from them. Fruit-tree wood is not soft, but it carves easily.

"Next year we are going to have a vegetable garden, and I think I'll get some goats. Most of my people are pretty definitely New York people, but I can draw them as well out here in Connecticut as I can in Manhattan, and we are thinking of living out here the whole year, rather than just for six months."

He comes to town every Tuesday with a bundle of drawings. His work appears most regularly in The

New Yorker, although he does illustrations for articles and stories in Collier's and other magazines. He has published a book, "Man About Town." He keeps no regular working hours, starting and knocking off when he pleases.

Right now he is turning out cartoons for a gasoline company in addition to his usual work, and on his weekly trip to the city he often comes across drawings of his pasted on Connecticut billboards.

His favorite comic strip is Barney Google, and when asked to name his favorite artists he mentioned Pieter Breughel and Giotto, who is said to have drawn a perfect circle with a single stroke when asked for a sample of his work to show a pope.

Asked to name some cartoonists whose work he respects, he began with James Thurber and named about twenty.

CHAPTER VIII

Showmanship

1. GEORGE BERNARD SHAW

*George Bernard Shaw Plays Hide-and-Seek, but Finally
Appears for the Press*

George Bernard Shaw fell today for one of the oldest gags used by the press photographers of the metropolis. From the time they boarded the Empress of Britain in the lower bay at 8 A.M. until an hour after it tied up at 10:30, news, sound and color photographers rushed frantically about the corridors looking for a chance to point their lenses at Shaw.

At 11 o'clock a self-confident cameraman rushed up to Shaw's stateroom 161 on A deck, and began to pound on the door. The startled face of Archibald Henderson appeared.

"I'm appealing to your sense of fair play," shouted the cameraman. "A little while ago three men got a shot at Shaw when he came up for breakfast. Now the rest of us are lost if he doesn't give us a break. Ask him to stand in the door for a moment. Appeal to his sense of fair play. Tell him we're appealing to his sense of fair play."

Mr. Henderson withdrew his startled face. In a moment Mr. Shaw looked out. His nose was sunburned. He rubbed it with a handkerchief on which he had rubbed medicine. He wore a green tie.

"Now, what's the matter out here?" he demanded.

Thirty photographers began to shout at once.

"My God," said Shaw. He walked out into the corridor.

"Wait a minute," he said, facing thirty cameras. "I'll go up on the sun deck."

The cameramen filled elevators, choked stairways. On the sun deck they hung to awning frames, shinnied up on ventilators.

On the deck Mr. Shaw stood against the railing and crossed his arms. A contact man for a sound-film company rushed up and asked him to wave his hand and say, "Hello boobs!"

"We thought that would be the kind of picture you would approve of," he said.

"How do you know what I approve of?" said Shaw. "I wish you'd throw all those cameras overboard. That's what I'd approve of," he said.

A cameraman began rolling. "Please turn this way, Mr. Shaw. Oh, Mr. Shaw! Oh, Mr. Shaw! For God's sake, tell the old fool to turn this way."

Mr. Shaw walked over to him and shook him by the shoulders. Red-faced, he shook the cameraman loose from his camera and a handful of plates. The crowd shouted, yelled, laughed. The other photographers busily exposed their plates.

Mr. Shaw had definite ideas on how he should pose for the movie cameras. The cameramen wanted a rail shot. Mr. Shaw insisted on a background of ventilator shafts. He would emerge from behind one and stroll toward the cameras.

His idea won, though before he could carry out the plan, he had to take a few more orders from the still cameramen. Finally, he got behind a ventilator. He straightened his tie and collar and stuck his hands in his pockets.

A cameraman shouted, "Now, Mr. Shaw is ready!" He was wrong, for Mr. Shaw said, "No, Mr. Shaw is not ready." "No, Mr. Shaw is not ready," the cameraman shouted.

He was wrong again. "Now I am ready," said Mr. Shaw, and out he came walking straight toward the cameras and looking very stern.

When he got near the cameras, he looked up and smiled broadly.

"I welcome you to America," said Archibald Henderson for the third time, shaking Mr. Shaw's hand for the benefit of the newsreel men.

"I am tired of being welcomed to America," said

Shaw. Abruptly, he turned his back on the battery and rushed for a stairway. The crowd, remembering his altercation with the photographer, cleared the way.

"No, I shall not say a word to newspapermen until tomorrow morning," said Shaw. "Don't you people understand English?"

You're Right, It's Shaw Finally Facing
Press Battery—and a Bit Testily

George Bernard Shaw sat in the smoking-room of the Empress of Britain at her pier today and kept his promise to talk freely to reporters after spending hours yesterday in efforts to evade them.

"Fire away, gentlemen," he said. "Occasionally you write ill-natured stories about things I haven't said. But fire away."

He was asked first about the reputed insult he offered Miss Helen Keller.

SHAW: The reporter who wrote the story should have been shot. All I told her was she could hear and speak and see much better than her countrymen.

Miss Keller wrote the story herself for The New York Times.

REPORTER: Would you be interested in a congress of the literary great to suppress war?

SHAW: Why should they suppress war? War is just

a method of killing people. There are a great many people who ought to be killed.

REPORTER: Do you think the English people ought to be killed?

Mr. Shaw declined to answer, gesturing as if he considered the question silly.

REPORTER: How about the Irish people?

SHAW: Yes, almost all the Irish should be killed.

Mr. Shaw said in his address last night at the Metropolitan Opera House that the real purpose of the American newspapers was to conceal the truth. He was asked to amplify.

SHAW: That's exactly what I mean. The newspapers get into the hands of big money, and whenever you write a story that is unfavorable to big money they do not waste time letting you know it.

REPORTER: I would like to tell you I think that isn't true.

SHAW: I am very amazed at your state of innocence.

REPORTER: What is your opinion of Henry L. Mencken?

SHAW: Mr. Mencken seems to have unusual intelligence for an American.

REPORTER: What do you think about Hitler?

SHAW: When a man opens his career as a politician with a persecution of the Jews, he is like an army officer starting his career cheating at cards. By the way, I understand you people tried to persecute the Catholics. Tell us, does the Ku Klux Klan still exist?

No one replied.

SHAW: Sometimes I stand amazed at the American people and wonder what will happen to them.

REPORTER: Do you think there is any hope of us changing?

SHAW: You better ask the Almighty about that.

REPORTER: I didn't know you had relations with the Almighty, Mr. Shaw.

SHAW: No, but the American people have.

REPORTER: Can you tell us one useful thing that your thirty volumes of plays have accomplished?

SHAW: All of them must have been some use to somebody.

REPORTER: Where do you think you will go when you die, Mr. Shaw?

SHAW: I sincerely hope when I die it will be the end of me. Do you think I am entertaining an eternity of George Bernard Shaw? How do you like the idea?

No one had an opinion.

REPORTER: What would you care to do or to see in New York if you stayed a little longer?

SHAW: Get out of it.

REPORTER: Do you enjoy making insulting remarks?

SHAW: Now, look here. If I say to an American, "You've got a hat on," he runs up and says, "See here, what do you mean saying I have a hat on?"

REPORTER: Do you think any of your plays will live a century?

SHAW: You never can tell about that. I've always said the sooner a reputation is done with the better. So long as the royalties last I will be satisfied.

WOMAN REPORTER: Would you like to go to the zoo, Mr. Shaw?

SHAW: I have a horror of the zoo. If I went to the zoo I would let out all the animals.

REPORTER: What do you think the next civilization will be?

SHAW: For all we know, the next civilization may be Negro.

REPORTER: Do you find humanity as stupid as you did when you were young?

SHAW: I look at the children leaving the schoolhouses. They seem to be the same old lot. I'm disappointed.

Thomas W. Lamont, who had heard Mr. Shaw say in his Opera House address that all financiers were 95 percent insane, accompanied Mr. Shaw to the boat in his automobile.

SHAW: His feelings didn't seem to be hurt.

REPORTER: What do you think of Eugene O'Neill?

SHAW: I didn't come here to say anything about my colleagues.

While reporters kept asking questions, Mr. Shaw reached into his pocket, brought out a watch, and said:

"I am through now. I have an appointment with my lawyer and my publisher."

He was sidetracked. Almost before he realized it, he found himself in the main lounge facing a battery of sound and still cameras. A dozen flashlight bulbs exploded at once. He stamped on the floor, raised his voice. "You mustn't suddenly explode them like that," he shouted. "And these microphones must be taken away."

He saw a newsreel man talking with Archibald Henderson. He went over and broke up the conversation.

"Now listen here," he said, "you are trying to get Mr. Henderson to welcome me to America again or some such silly thing, and I won't have it. Move those microphones out of here!"

Suddenly Mr. Shaw wheeled around and faced the microphones. He grabbed two of them and hauled them aside. One fell over and upset a long line of wires. In another part of the room a machine began clicking.

"Will you please stop that microphone!" he yelled. "What's that noise over there?"

"That's a sound camera, chief," said a cameraman. "It's all right."

Mr. Shaw expressed disapproval of the chairs in which he and Professor Henderson were asked to sit. The Professor began moving them off the floor.

"He wants you to walk up and I will get out of a chair and shake hands with you," said Mr. Shaw. "What nonsense! I won't do it. What are those for, those things over there? Are they microphones? All right, I'm leaving."

He left the floor hurriedly. Professor Henderson followed, trying to persuade him to return.

"Hell, I told Queen Marie to pull up her dress," said a cameraman. "This guy doesn't bother me. If he wants to come back, O.K. If he doesn't, let him stay in his hole."

Before Shaw got into his stateroom a woman reporter stopped him, asked a question about the Scottsboro case.

"Blow the Scottsboro boys!" he shouted, slamming the door. "I didn't come here to interfere with your silly laws."

Mr. Shaw called the American Constitution "a charter of anarchy" in his speech last night.

"I meant just that," he said today. "It should be set aside. It is merely an accumulation of efforts on the part of a people to escape governing themselves. I realize that in this world it is a difficult matter to be free. I want to be free, but I can't be free the whole time. If we cannot have complete freedom, we can have it within limits and escape the present tyranny of laws no one wants."

Mr. Shaw, turning to another phase of the speech last night, said, "I did not mention William Jennings Bryan to illustrate the perfect example of a 100 percent American. He was a magnificent man, an enormous man who spent his life on the issue of silver, which he thought would change the world and improve the entire human race. I did not mention him, but I might readily have done so."

Mr. Shaw pretended he could not understand American interest in him.

"Why, for instance," he asked, "are you all around me here? It is admiration of a sort, but why? If you had read my books I could understand it, but few people who say they admire me have read my books or know anything about me except what they read in the newspapers.

"I am interested in this abstract longing, your sense of admiration, and only wish that it could be turned into a direction that were sensible. Perhaps I should say that you people are filled with unemployed emotions."

It was suggested his books were widely read.

"What?" Shaw replied. "You have not met nonreaders of Shaw books who admire Shaw? Then you have met the wrong people. There are stacks of people whose eyes fill with tears when you mention Bernard Shaw."

Mr. Shaw told Lawrence Langner, of the board of managers of the Theatre Guild, which has produced many Shaw plays, that he had other plays in contemplation. Mr. Langner, his wife, Armina Marshall, Robert Lorraine and the Princess Kropotkin were Shaw's breakfast guests aboard ship.

Only six persons grew tired and left last night as Shaw stood behind a great basket of flowers on the stage of the Opera House and spoke 16,000 critical words in 100 minutes. He was applauded vigorously as he berated almost every American institution. The audience displayed more laughter than applause when he said America might possibly save the world.

Mr. Shaw declared that President Roosevelt's four years, "if he has to go on under the Constitution with the usual rotten Congress and all the rest of it," will inevitably be as great a disappointment as Mr. Hoover's administration.

He said the smallest smattering of the knowledge of political science would teach us that the first thing to do to get out of the present mess is to nationalize banks.

*Shaw, 80 and "Dying," Reneges at His Works Being
Entombed in Textbooks*

George Bernard Shaw, who hates birthdays almost
as much as he hates beef, beer, tobacco smoke and
Americans, will be eighty tomorrow, but it is doubtful if he will celebrate the occasion because, as he
once told a reporter, "public interest in me depends
on things I can do that nobody else can, and anybody
can have a birthday."

The celebrated vegetarian, playwright and wise-
cracker is in sound health except for an occasional
cold, according to one of his American representa-
tives, Howard C. Lewis of Dodd, Mead & Company.
And to judge from one of his letters, an explosive
letter which Mr. Lewis decided to make public today,
Mr. Shaw still is in possession of the acrid wit which
has made him one of the firebrands of English letters.

The letter has to do with sections of the contract
between the publishers and Mr. Shaw concerning
school editions, anthology reprints and fees for producing his plays.

"I will have nothing to do with schools and col-
leges at any price; no book of mine shall, with my
consent, ever be that damnable thing, a schoolbook,"
wrote Mr. Shaw. "Let them buy the dollar editions if
they want them. By a school edition they mean an
edition with notes and prefaces full of material for

such questions as, 'Give the age of Bernard Shaw's great-aunt when he wrote "You Never Can Tell" and state the reason for believing that the inscription on her tomb at Ballyhooly is incorrect.' The experienced students read the notes and prefaces and not the plays and forever after loathe my very name."

Mr. Shaw wrote that when he is asked for permission to include one of his plays in an anthology, "it is my custom to blackmail the publisher to the extent of a donation to the Society of Authors or the Authors' League of America."

He said amateur fees (for producing his plays) were hardly worth collecting and that he was in the habit of allowing little theaters professional fees (5 percent on the gross receipts when they do not exceed $250), "providing they constitute themselves permanently and keep all the money they make in the concern, instead of giving it away to charities, or else getting drunk with it in the regular professional way."

Mr. Shaw also had several personal things to say in discussing the length of his agreement with the publishing house.

"The limit of five years probably will be quite forgotten by us, as the agreement goes on automatically to all eternity if we are satisfied with it," he wrote. "But if Frank [Frank Dodd, president of Dodd, Mead] goes mad, and Edward [Edward Dodd, chairman of the board] and Chase [Arthur Chase, trea-

surer] are hanged, and Lewis takes to publishing pornographic literature and is Comstocked for it, how
am I to get out unless I can break at six months' notice? Besides, you may want to get rid of me in case
I become too infamous for any respectable publisher
to touch me."

Mr. Lewis said that, on the eve of the playwright's
eightieth birthday, he would like to make an attempt
to eradicate the impression, widespread in the United
States, that Mr. Shaw is "mercenary, dollar-mad and
penny-pinching."

"I hope he will have an extremely pleasant birthday," said Mr. Lewis, "because I admire him. In 1933
I went to London to ask him to change publishers, to
change from Brentano's to Dodd, Mead. I went to
see him at his home, 4 Whitehall Court, and he got
to talking. We talked for hours about Russia, about
foreign sections in New York, about the Comstock
laws, and things as disparate as that. Finally his secretary rushed in and said I would have to go. Shaw told
me to come back the next day.

"The next visit the same thing happened. Shaw
talked and talked and we never got around to the business of changing publishers and writing out a contract. Just before I left Shaw said, 'Well, we haven't
had time to talk about the contract, but I'll tell you
what I'll do, I'll write one out tonight and send it to

you.' The next morning a messenger arrived at my hotel, the Savoy, with the contract.

"It was in his handwriting and it was an absolutely satisfactory and fair arrangement. It was the fairest contract I ever saw and as legal as any lawyer could make it. It was a complicated contract, because the matter was involved, but he made it clear as water. I had heard that Shaw was mercenary, and I was surprised at the absolute fairness of the paper. With it was a note asking me to send him a copy of the contract when I got back to the United States. When an author, especially one with the reputation for shrewdness that Shaw has, trusts a publisher to that extent, it is news."

Since his seventy-ninth birthday Mr. Shaw has uttered a few more of his customarily straightforward pronouncements. Informed of the death of Robert Loraine, the famous British actor, he said, "I cannot sympathize about his death because I am going to die myself shortly." The biggest ruction he stirred up during the year involved a postcard he wrote to the Children's Aid Society of London, which had asked him to support one of their charities. (Mr. Shaw's attitude toward charity is unbending; he describes it as "a pernicious evasion of public duty.")

"As the world at present is not fit for children to live in," Mr. Shaw scribbled on the back of the postcard, "why not give the little invalids a gorgeous party and then, when they have eaten and danced themselves to sleep, turn on the gas and let them all wake up in heaven?"

Judging from this polite missive, the cranky vegetarian is not getting to be a softy in his old age.

2. Gene Krupa Wants to "Swing African"

Night and day in a hot soundproof room in the Brunswick Building, Gene Krupa is whacking a new band of swing musicians in shape for a tour. Gene Krupa is a skinny, shambling young man with long fingers and the grin of a happy maniac, who began messing with a trap drum while jerking soda in a "dime-grind" resort on a river outside Madison, Wisconsin, and is now, fourteen summers later, considered the best drummer in the world. He left Benny Goodman a few weeks ago and organized a band of his own, selecting his men from bands all over.

"I got certain ideas about music I couldn't carry out with Goodman," said Mr. Krupa. "I wanted to go further. There was an expedition to Africa that made some recordings of drummers in the Congo jungle, and I got hold of them, twelve sides of them, and I've been studying them. Those boys know how to drum. They tell me I know something about beating a drum, and I guess I do, but those boys can sure handle a drum. I want to get some of that stuff, that genuine African drumming, into my band. Right out of the jungle, you might say."

Most jazz drummers fit out their drums with so many noise-making accessories they look more like a college boy's automobile than a drum, a habit Mr. Krupa despises. "Just give me a drum," he said. "I knock all that stuff off. Had my way I'd just take a barrel and stretch two heads over it and let it dry in the sun, and I'd have me a drum. I got a lot of drums. I could take my drums and move into a vacant store, and I would be open for business. I got eight snares and six bass drums, and fifteen tomtoms. I got five or six trunks of traps. I'm always busting a drum. Other men may think different; I think a drum is the foundation of a band."

While Mr. Krupa talked his men kept on playing. He has three trumpets, four saxophones, a guitar, a piano player, a bass, and himself. When he left Mr. Goodman he went around the country and picked up men whose playing he had heard and admired. He has worked with at least eight bands—"everything from little old hole-in-the-wall bands to the big name bands"—and every time on tour he heard playing he liked, he wrote the player's name down in a notebook he carries.

"When I got ready to start my band," he said, "I

knew just who I wanted in it. I had all the names in my black book. All I did, I just went around the country and signed them up. Two I got from the Coast, and two from Detroit, and some came from Texas. The rest from just around. We have forty-eight arrangements now but I want sixty before we start. We open in Atlantic City and then they have us booked ahead two months, all one-night stands. Once a week we come into New York to make records. The tour is training, kind of. I want us to be good before we open up in New York."

Except for jerking soda, beating a drum is the only work Mr. Krupa has ever done. He was born in Chicago. He is twenty-nine. His father, Bartley Krupa, was a South Side alderman, who died when Gene was around eight. His name is Austrian—"I'd say it was Austrian," he said, "but my mother was a Swede." He started to study for the priesthood at a school in Indiana, working in the summer as a soda jerker.

"I would stand next to the icebox and open up these cold drinks, these nickel drinks," he said. "It wasn't really soda jerking. Mostly bottle stuff. They had a band, and the drummer used to let me fool around with his drum. I got so I could play a little, and he'd let me sit in. He was glad to get a rest. Well, you know the way those things happen—he got sick, and they took me on. When we closed up at the Wisconsin Beach Gardens, I moved up to Chicago and joined the union and got in a band. Since then I've been drumming."

He is married to Ethel Fawcett. She used to be a telephone operator at the Dixie Hotel. For amusement he goes to ball games and reads sports news. He said, however, that about the only thing he is interested in is drumming. When he was with Goodman, swing fans used to gather around him and exhibit signs of insanity as the sticks he threw into the air came to rest unerringly in his fingers, and as his sticks flew from rattling cymbal to snare to cowbell to tomtom. He is happy when swing fans gather around him and jump up and down.

"I like to see them go crazy," he said. "I sure do."

2. George M. Cohan

"Yeah, I used to like to hang around Broadway and drink beer with the boys," said George M. Cohan, looking from the window of his apartment on Fifth Avenue to the fat, noisy pigeons roosting in the eaves of the Metropolitan Museum across the street.

"Now I hardly ever see the street. I mean, sometimes I pass it on the way to my lawyer's office, or going downtown to play a part, or sometimes I drop into Dinty Moore's for some liver and bacon and a couple of rye highballs, but I don't exactly feel it's the same town I used to live in any more.

"Whenever I feel like drinking, I go down to the Plaza, the old Plaza, where they have this rack of horse cabs in front, but I don't even do that much any more. All I do is go for rides in Central Park, usually around the Reservoir, and I don't miss many ball games, although I don't root for any particular club.

"Walking around town isn't as much fun as it used to be; my old pal Steve Reardon, the retired policeman, is dead now, and I used to get a kick out of walking with him. Funny guy. Used to like to walk a lot. Used to ship his grip up to Albany when the seasons changed and start walking toward his grip. When spring came he would put some money in his sock and start walking toward his grip."

Mr. Cohan's career as a song-and-dance man, as a playwright-actor-producer, as songwriter and as an ill-fated movie star has been distinguished by the range and quality of his indignation, but he said the brassy state of Broadway does not make him indignant; it merely makes him want to stay home. His quarrelsomeness has been monumental ever since the days when the Four Cohans used to be chosen instead of a stable of acrobats to open a vaudeville ball, occasions when his mother, father and sister had to restrain him from leaving the theater. At the close of almost every vaudeville engagement he used to rush up to the manager of the theater and shout, "Sometime I'm going to come back here and buy this theater just so I can throw you into the street."

He will oblige any reporter with a blast against Hollywood—"If I had my choice between Hollywood and Atlanta, I'd take Leavenworth," or something like that—but concerning Broadway he is sorrowful, not outraged. He is a little like the man who saves up enough money for a trip to his hometown and finds that all the people he used to know are not there any more.

"They have to make a living too," he says when he walks down Broadway and stares at the auctioneers and strongman professors in every second store, and the barkers with megaphones yelling their heads off in front of dime-a-head movie palaces. He does not forget that there was a lot of trash on the old Broadway when he walks through the territories in the theatrical district so flashy and noisy they make Coney Island resemble an elegant watering place on the Riviera.

"Oh, sure," he said, speaking out of the right corner of his twisted mouth, "things have got to move on, and change and grow old. There's a lot of good stuff in the American theater, even in Hollywood. W. C. Fields, for example, an artist if there ever was one, and Groucho Marx, and this young man Clifford Odets is all right. He reeks of the theater. He pounds on the table a lot, but he's good. When I was seeing 'Awake and Sing' there were times when I couldn't sit still."

He is going to open up in "a little comedy" around Thanksgiving, when the elections are over, and he's going to take it on the road. He hasn't written any campaign songs this year, and does not plan to. He has not forgotten that a lot of people laughed when they heard his 1934 song for Roosevelt, "What a man, what a man, what a ma-a-an," sung to the tune of his most famous song, "Over There." (For the Jubilee of Light he wrote a similar song concerning Thomas Alva Edison, "What a man, what a plan," sung to the same tune.) He also said that he does not think that he will wave the American flag during this election. He has been a Democrat all his life, but this election he appears to be a little puzzled.

"I've got friends in both places," he said.

In two years Mr. Cohan will be sixty, but he says that the muscles in his legs would still stand a three-a-day vaudeville tour. His hair is white, but his pink face is amazingly youthful.

"I may not look it, but sometimes I feel my age," he said. "However, I keep myself in good condition walking. I weigh 136. I didn't weigh 100 until I was twenty-seven.

"In the season of 1927–28 I danced for thirty-seven weeks. For thirteen years I hadn't danced a lick, and this old actor, Arthur Deagon, dropped dead on me, and I jumped in and took his part with no trouble. That was in 'The Merry Malones.' It is good to know that your muscles aren't asleep. I can't play golf or tennis, or any of the things most regular guys can do. I can't even swim, and I've never learned how to drive an automobile. I'm probably the only person left in the world who doesn't know how to drive.

"I take it out walking. There is a cult of people who take daily walks around the Reservoir. Why, I see more people I know by face, walking in Central Park—people you can speak to and say, 'Hello there, how are you?'—than I see on Broadway.

"I don't drink much any more. I haven't had a dozen drinks in the last six months. I was in Europe twelve weeks this summer and I didn't take a single drink, no stout in Ireland, no wine in France. I'm not on the wagon or anything. I don't stand on ceremony with myself—when I feel like a few drinks I go downtown and get them."

His trip to Ireland last summer was something he had promised himself for many years. He made a sedate tour through Leinster and Munster, not venturing into the North. His grandparents were from Cork, and he had a good time there. He went to see the Lakes of Killarney in County Kerry, and watched the Liffey flowing into the Irish Sea at Dublin, a quiet trip with his wife, looking at places he had heard about all his life. His son, George Michael Harris Cohan, is now working for a lithographer, although Mr. Cohan used to say he wanted him to be a ballplayer. Mr. Cohan shows up at a ball park every day there is a game in the city.

"According to the gossip around town," he said, "I have tried to buy every ball club in both leagues. One time I did buy the New York Giants with Sam Harris, my partner. We shook hands on the deal and I thought the matter was settled, but another offer came up next morning and the owners forgot they shook hands with Sam Harris and George Cohan and sold it to the new fellow."

Mr. Cohan does not have an office any more. His hat is his office, although he keeps an account in the office of Sam Harris, his old partner.

"I also have a storehouse on some street in the Fifties," he said. "Which street it is I've forgotten. There are two lofts full of my old sets and lighting equipment and costumes. I haven't been in that storehouse in years. I bet it would cost me $5,000 to move all that stuff over to Long Island City, and burn it."

Mr. Cohan said that the story that he intended to leave Broadway for good and troupe with an Ohio and Mississippi River showboat was a good story, but that Charles Washburn, the press agent, was responsible for it.

"You give a press agent a pencil and no telling what he will do," said Mr. Cohan. "This old show-boat producer in Cincinnati, Billy Bryant, happened to be a friend of Mr. Washburn's and he got me to let him write Bryant saying I wanted a job. Bryant had just written a book and Charlie wanted to get him some publicity."

The letter to the river producer, ostensibly from Mr. Cohan, contained this tear-jerking paragraph: "Can you use another good song-and-dance man this summer? I want to be a child again and play hookey from the skeptic applause of the dry-land theater. I've missed something in life, and I want to get away from the hardships of writing, acting and producing plays for the Broadway of today."

"It was a good letter," said Mr. Cohan, shedding a couple of tears, "and I wish I could compose like that. Anyway, I wouldn't mind acting in a few old-time melodramas again. I remember trouping with a thriller called 'Daniel Boone on the Trail.' It was so melodramatic at times that they often had to pump blood out of the cellar before they could finish the third act."

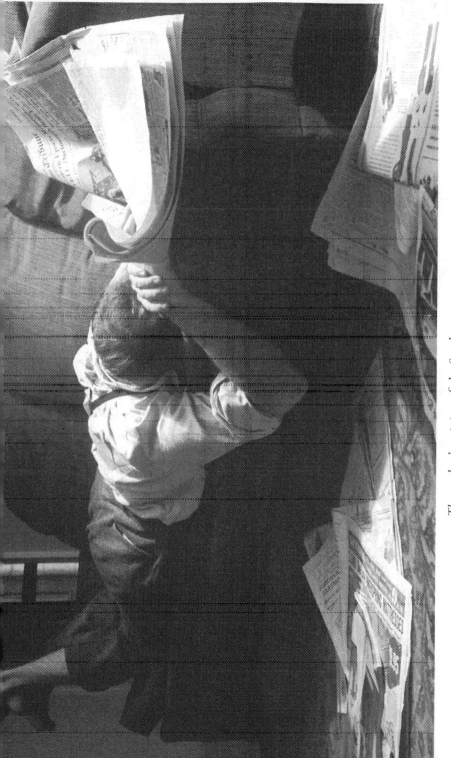

The author's opinion of the Sunday newspaper